To Melinda,

Look forward to a tasting session!

Love

Gillian x

acarons

+ Medium Egg whites (Separate

Icing Sugar   170g

ground almonds 160g

water 50ml

granulated Sugar 160g

bake at   150°C fan (160°C)

THE BOY WHO BAKES

EDD KIMBER

KYLE BOOKS

PHOTOGRAPHY BY YUKI SUGIURA

TO MY MUM AND DAD, WHO HAVE ALWAYS SUPPORTED
ME AND ENCOURAGED ME TO FOLLOW MY PASSION

First published in Great Britain in 2011 by
Kyle Books
23 Howland Street
London, W1T 4AY
general.enquiries@kylebooks.com
www.kylebooks.com

ISBN: 978-0-85783-045-6

Text © 2011 Edd Kimber
Photographs © 2011 Yuki Sugiura
Design © 2011 Kyle Books

Editor: Catharine Robertson
Typography: Georgia Vaux
Photographer: Yuki Sugiura
Props stylist: Cynthia Inions
Food stylists: Bianca Nice and Edd Kimber
Copy editor: Jan Cutler
Production: David Hearn and Nic Jones

A Cataloguing In Publication record for this
title is available from the British Library.

Colour reproduction by Alta Image
Printed and bound in Italy
by Printer Trento S.r.l.

INTRODUCTION

For me, baking is cooking at its most fun. You take the simplest of ingredients, such as eggs, flour, sugar and butter, and turn them into something amazing, like a triple-layer red velvet cake, which you can then share with those you love. And that's the other reason I enjoy baking: it's an extension of love. Rarely do you bake solely for yourself; it's normally to share with people who are special to you.

My passion for baking started when I was a child. My dad comes from Yorkshire and my mum comes from Lancashire, so I grew up surrounded by quite traditional and old-fashioned baking, and I loved it all. I remember standing on a stool in the kitchen one Christmas cutting out rounds of pastry for the mincepies; I remember learning to make scones with my mum; I remember my grandma teaching me to bake bread. These memories have always stayed with me and still inspire me today. But as my interest in baking grew, so did my imagination and appetite to try new ideas and new flavours.

What really turned me into a baker was competing in *The Great British Bake Off* in 2010. I was stuck in a rut in my job, having nothing at all creative to do. At that time baking was my escape, and I would spend all day thinking up new recipes or exciting flavour combinations. I decided to take a chance and entered the BBC show, never expecting to even get an audition. Over 4000 people applied, but I was chosen as a contestant, and after over six weeks of challenges I came out on top. It was just the push I needed to follow my dreams and properly pursue my lifelong passion for baking.

I wanted this book to represent the whole of that fantastic and very personal journey, so I have included lots recipes based on ones from my childhood, some of which have been passed down through generations of my family. I rediscovered many of these in the family recipe box while writing this book. But although the original recipes are traditional, expect to find the odd twist here and there in my versions. I have also created recipes that really represent me now: they're modern, playful and definitely don't take themselves too seriously. There are simple recipes and others that are more challenging, but all are completely achievable. Above all, I hope they will inspire you to get into the kitchen and have a go because, perhaps most importantly, baking is fun and very, very tasty. Enjoy!

USEFUL EQUIPMENT

If you're just starting to bake you can get by with a few simple basics such as baking trays, bowls, whisks, a muffin tray and cake tins, kitchen scales and a rolling pin, but if you want to take your baking further there are some pieces of equipment that will make your life much easier and help you get even better results.

BAKING TRAYS

I prefer to use heavy-duty light-coloured baking trays, which can be bought inexpensively from restaurant supply shops and kitchenware shops. Cheap, dark and flimsy baking trays tend to bake unevenly and brown the base of baked foods too quickly, whereas these bake more evenly.

BAKING BEANS

You can buy ceramic baking beans for blind baking pastry in most kitchenware shops, and they work wonderfully, but you can also use rice or dried pulses just as easily. Set aside a bag and you can use them time and time again.

BROWNIE/TRAYBAKE TINS

Just as for baking trays, I prefer to use light-coloured metal or even glass brownie and traybake tins. Dark tins overbake the bases and edges. Almost all of the recipes in this book use a standard 23 × 33cm tin.

CAKE AND LOAF TINS

Most of the recipes in the cake chapter use standard 20cm round tins. Don't use old-fashioned sandwich tins, which can be too shallow – they need to be about 5cm deep. All the loaf cakes in this book use standard 23 × 10cm loaf tins. As with all baking tins, choose heavy-duty light-coloured metal versions.

COOKIE CUTTERS

Only a few of my recipes use cookie cutters, and for that purpose a small set of plain round cutters in multiple sizes will do the job perfectly. They are also useful for making templates for macarons and cutting out rounds of pastry.

ELECTRIC MIXERS

I use my electric freestanding mixer almost every day and I don't regret buying it for a minute. It makes baking so much more efficient and easy: no more whipping egg whites by hand, or creaming butter and sugar together for what seems like days. If you love baking, I recommend buying an electric freestanding mixer, or at least an electric hand mixer. I suggest using the paddle attachment in a freestanding mixer to make the cake batters in this book.

FOOD PROCESSOR

Although not strictly required, there are certain recipes, such as the Hazelnut and Chocolate Macarons (page 65) which might be difficult to make without a food processor. They are also great for making pastry.

ICE CREAM MAKER To make ice cream that has the best texture you need to use some form of ice cream maker. They come in all sorts of sizes and prices. If you only make ice cream occasionally, there is no reason to buy an expensive electric model; get yourself a cheap model that uses a pre-frozen chamber.

ICE CREAM SCOOPS I find ice cream scoops perfect for forming cookies into rounds and measuring cupcake batter into moulds. It makes baking more accurate – and faster too.

MEASURING SPOONS When a recipe calls for a teaspoon of baking powder it means a level teaspoon, which is an accurate 5ml measure. You can't get this accuracy with the teaspoon you use to make your cup of tea, so it's worth investing in a set of measuring spoons. Most supermarkets sell them very cheaply.

MIXING BOWLS I prefer to use a set of Pyrex bowls for baking because they are cheap, heatproof and durable – just what you need for baking. I prefer not to use plastic, as they tend to retain a film of fat even after being washed carefully.

MUFFIN TRAY For this book you will only need one standard-sized muffin tray with 12 cups, but if you make a lot of cupcakes or muffins, having two would make a lot of sense. Try to stick to heavy-duty and light-coloured versions so that your cakes will bake nice and evenly.

OFFSET SPATULA Apart from buying a cake turntable, an offset spatula is the best utensil I can suggest to make decorating cakes easier. Spreading frosting across the tops and sides of cakes is much simpler using one of these, as it gives you more control, and makes it easier to get a flat surface.

PIPING BAGS These are invaluable for piping out macaron batter into perfect little rounds and are also useful for piping choux pastry to make eclairs. I prefer to use the disposable type – it makes for much easier cleaning up.

SUGAR THERMOMETER Where a recipe indicates that a sugar syrup has to be cooked to a specific temperature, a sugar thermometer is needed to achieve this accuracy. They are cheap and easy to get hold of; many supermarkets stock them.

TART TINS All the individual tartlets in the pastry chapter are made using tins that are 10cm in diameter, with removable bases. All the full-sized tarts use a 23cm tin, again with a removable base.

CAKES

MY ULTIMATE CHOCOLATE CAKE

This cake is a family recipe brought back from Canada by my mum, whilst she was visiting relatives in her twenties. Unfortunately, it was never actually made until I rediscovered it in the family recipe box many years later, which is a great shame as I was a huge fan of chocolate cake as a child. One of my earliest memories is of the day my older sister decided to make a chocolate cake with my twin brother and me. I loved it, but I'm not sure how impressed our mum was when she came back to find her two boys under the table covered in chocolate after licking the bowl clean!

SERVES 12–16

110G UNSALTED BUTTER, AT ROOM TEMPERATURE, PLUS EXTRA FOR GREASING

110G PLAIN CHOCOLATE (AT LEAST 60–70% COCOA SOLIDS)

280ML BOILING WATER

3 TABLESPOONS COCOA POWDER

140ML BUTTERMILK

280G PLAIN FLOUR

2 TEASPOONS BICARBONATE OF SODA

½ TEASPOON SALT

340G SOFT BROWN SUGAR

2 TEASPOONS VANILLA EXTRACT

3 EGGS, LIGHTLY BEATEN

FOR THE GANACHE

225G BUTTER

285G PLAIN CHOCOLATE (AT LEAST 60–70% COCOA SOLIDS)

2 TABLESPOONS GOLDEN SYRUP

240ML DOUBLE CREAM

Preheat the oven to 180°C (160°C fan oven) gas mark 4. Grease and line three 20cm round cake tins with baking parchment, then grease the parchment too. Melt the chocolate in a microwave or a heatproof bowl over a pan of gently simmering water, making sure the base of the bowl doesn't touch the water. Set aside to cool slightly. In a medium bowl, whisk the water and cocoa powder together, then whisk in the buttermilk and set aside.

Sift the flour, bicarbonate of soda and salt together into a medium bowl. In a separate bowl use an electric hand mixer to beat the butter, sugar and vanilla together until light and fluffy, about 5 minutes. Beat in the eggs, a little at a time, beating until fully combined. With the mixer on low pour the cooled chocolate down the side of the bowl and, once fully combined, add a third of the flour mixture followed by half the buttermilk mixture. Repeat and then add the final third of flour mixture. Divide equally among the three prepared tins and bake for 25–30 minutes or until a cocktail stick inserted into the centre comes out clean. Cool in the tins for 10 minutes before inverting onto wire racks to cool completely.

To make the ganache, melt the butter, chocolate and golden syrup in the microwave or a heatproof bowl over a pan of gently simmering water, making sure the base of the bowl doesn't touch the water. Once melted and smooth, add the cream and mix to combine. Remove from the heat and allow to set until spreadable, about 15–20 minutes. If the ganache is not setting at room temperature you can refrigerate, but watch carefully that it stays spreadable.

To assemble the cake, put the first layer of cake on a serving plate or cake board. Spread a layer of ganache over the top of the cake and put the second cake layer on top, then repeat. Put the final layer of cake on top and spread the remaining ganache over the top and sides of the cake. Decorate with anything you fancy. Here I've used sprinkles for a classic birthday cake look.

RASPBERRY RIPPLE CAKE

This cake came about when I offered to make my boyfriend a birthday cake in any flavour. I was expecting him to say chocolate or lemon, something more run-of-the-mill, but was thrown a little curve ball with a request for raspberry ripple. The resulting cake went down a real treat – my take on his favourite childhood ice cream flavour.

SERVES 12–16

335G BUTTER, PLUS EXTRA FOR GREASING

335G PLAIN FLOUR

3 TEASPOONS BAKING POWDER

400G CASTER SUGAR

6 EGGS, SEPARATED

2 TEASPOONS VANILLA EXTRACT

185ML WHOLE MILK

80G RASPBERRY JAM, FOR COATING THE LAYERS

FOR THE WHITE CHOCOLATE FROSTING

80G WHITE CHOCOLATE

250G GRANULATED SUGAR

5 LARGE EGG WHITES

450G UNSALTED BUTTER

80G RASPBERRY JAM, SIEVED

Preheat the oven to 180°C (160°C fan oven) gas mark 4 and lightly grease three 20cm round cake tins and line with baking parchment, then grease the parchment too. Sift the flour and baking powder into a medium bowl. Using an electric mixer, beat the butter and 300g of the sugar until light and fluffy, about 5 minutes. Beat in the egg yolks one at a time, followed by the vanilla. Turn the mixer to low and add a third of the flour mixture followed by half the milk. Repeat and then add the final third of flour mixture.

Put the egg whites into a clean bowl and whisk until they form soft peaks. Increase the speed and slowly add the remaining sugar, whisking until they hold stiff and glossy peaks. Gradually fold the egg mixture into the cake batter. Divide equally among the three tins, level with a spatula and bake for 30–35 minutes or until a cocktail stick inserted into the centre comes out clean. Cool in the tins for 10 minutes before inverting onto a wire rack to cool completely.

For the frosting, melt the chocolate in a microwave or a heatproof bowl over a pan of gently simmering water, making sure the base of the bowl doesn't touch the water. Allow to cool. Put 160ml water and the sugar into a pan over medium heat. Bring to the boil and have a sugar thermometer ready. Meanwhile, put the egg whites into a clean bowl (this is best done using a freestanding electric mixer) and whisk on medium. As the syrup reaches about 115°C start whisking the egg whites on high. Once the syrup reaches 121°C, remove it from the heat and, with the mixer still running, slowly pour the syrup down the side of the bowl, avoiding the whisk. Continue whisking on high speed until the meringue has cooled to room temperature.

With the mixer on medium-high speed, gradually add the butter, until fully combined. Once the frosting is smooth and fluffy, divide it into two bowls, mixing the chocolate into one and the jam into the other. To assemble the cake, put one layer on a plate or cake board and spread with half the raspberry jam, then top with a third of the white chocolate frosting. Repeat with the second cake layer, placing the final layer of cake on top. Spread the top and sides of the cake with the raspberry frosting. To create the swirl effect, spread the remaining white chocolate frosting across random sections of the cake.

CARAMEL AND CINNAMON CAKE

This is all about showcasing my favourite ingredient: caramel. The cinnamon in the cake complements the caramel in the filling and frosting, creating a flavour that is just delicious — perfect for afternoon tea. The cake is light and airy because it is made a little differently from usual. Rather then creaming the butter and sugar, the eggs and sugar are warmed, then whisked vigorously until they increase in volume.

SERVES 12–16

40G UNSALTED BUTTER, MELTED AND COOLED, PLUS EXTRA FOR GREASING

8 LARGE EGGS

180G LIGHT BROWN SUGAR

100G DARK BROWN SUGAR

200G PLAIN FLOUR

20G CORNFLOUR

2 TEASPOONS GROUND CINNAMON

1 TEASPOON FRESHLY GRATED NUTMEG

90G WALNUTS, ROUGHLY CHOPPED

FOR THE ITALIAN MERINGUE FROSTING

250G GRANULATED SUGAR

5 LARGE EGG WHITES

450G UNSALTED BUTTER

1 QUANTITY SALTED CARAMEL SAUCE (PAGE 153)

Preheat the oven to 180°C (160°C fan oven) gas mark 4. Grease and line three 20cm round cake tins with baking parchment, then grease the parchment too. In a large heatproof bowl, lightly whisk the eggs and sugars together. Put the bowl over a medium pan of simmering water and whisk until the sugar has dissolved. Remove the bowl from the heat and beat on medium-high speed until the mixture forms a slowly dissolving ribbon when the whisk is lifted out.

Mix the flour, cornflour, cinnamon and nutmeg into a bowl. Sift a third of the flour mixture over the egg mixture and gently fold. Repeat twice more with the remaining flour mixture, folding lightly until just combined. Beat a large spoonful of batter into the melted butter, then fold this mixture back into the remaining batter. Divide the batter among the tins and bake for 15–20 minutes or until a cocktail stick inserted into the centre comes out clean. Remove the cakes from the oven and let them cool in their tins. Run a knife around the edge of the cakes and invert onto wire racks. Peel off the baking parchment.

For the frosting, put 160ml water and the sugar into a pan set over medium heat. Bring to the boil and have a sugar thermometer ready. Meanwhile, put the egg whites into a clean bowl (this is best done using a freestanding electric mixer) and whisk on medium. As the syrup reaches about 115°C start whisking the egg whites on high. Once the syrup has reached 121°C, remove it from the heat and, with the mixer still running, pour the syrup in a slow stream down the side of the bowl, avoiding the whisk. Continue whisking on high speed until the meringue has cooled to room temperature. With the mixer on medium-high speed, add the butter, a few pieces at a time, beating until fully combined. Add about two-thirds of the caramel sauce and beat to combine.

To assemble the cake, put one cake layer onto a serving plate or cake board and drizzle with a little of the caramel and a third of the chopped walnuts. Spread the layer with a large dollop of the frosting. Repeat with the second cake layer, placing the final layer of cake on top. Spread the sides and top of the cake with the remaining frosting. To decorate, sprinkle the remaining walnuts around the edge and drizzle the remaining caramel across the top.

APPLE PIE CAKE

An apple pie or a cake? I couldn't decide which, so I came up with this cake — a cross between the two. I have taken the flavours of the classic pie and transformed it into a spectacular three-layered cake. This cake is best served as soon as it is assembled, so if you want to prepare it ahead of time you can make the cakes and, once cooled, wrap them in clingfilm, making the fillings just before they are needed.

SERVES 12–16

225G UNSALTED BUTTER, AT ROOM
    TEMPERATURE, PLUS EXTRA FOR
    GREASING
470G PLAIN FLOUR
4 TEASPOONS BAKING POWDER
½ TEASPOON SALT
3 TEASPOONS GROUND CINNAMON
¼ TEASPOON NUTMEG
400G CASTER SUGAR
4 LARGE EGGS, SEPARATED
1 TEASPOON VANILLA BEAN PASTE
250ML WHOLE MILK

FOR THE CINNAMON CREAM
    CHEESE FROSTING
110G UNSALTED BUTTER
250G ICING SUGAR
200G CREAM CHEESE (FULL FAT)
½ TEASPOON VANILLA EXTRACT
½ TEASPOON GROUND CINNAMON

FOR THE CARAMELISED APPLES
5–6 GRANNY SMITH APPLES
85G UNSALTED BUTTER
85G LIGHT BROWN SUGAR
½ TEASPOON GROUND GINGER

Preheat the oven to 170°C (150°C fan oven) gas mark 3. Grease three 20cm round cake tins and line the bases with baking parchment, then grease these too. Sift the flour, baking powder, salt and cinnamon together into a medium bowl, then set aside. Using an electric mixer, beat the butter and 300g of the sugar until light and fluffy, about 5 minutes. Beat in the egg yolks one at a time, beating until fully combined, followed by the vanilla bean paste. Turn the mixer to low and add a third of the flour mixture followed by half the milk. Repeat and then add the final third of flour mixture.

Put the egg whites into a clean, grease-free bowl and whisk until they hold soft peaks, then increase the speed and slowly pour in the remaining sugar, whisking the eggs until stiff peaks form. Mix a large spoonful of the egg white mixture into the cake batter to lighten it, then gently fold in the remaining whites, until just fully combined. Divide the batter equally among the three tins, level out with a spatula and bake for 30–35 minutes or until a cocktail stick inserted into the centre of the cake comes out clean. Cool in the tins for 10 minutes before inverting onto a wire rack to cool completely.

To make the frosting, use an electric mixer to beat the butter until light and smooth, about 5 minutes. Slowly beat in the icing sugar until combined, then increase the speed and beat until light and fluffy. Beat in the cream cheese. To make the caramelised apples, core, quarter and dice the apples, then add to a large pan with the butter, sugar and ginger. Cook over medium heat until the apples are tender and coated in caramel. Drain the apples, reserving the juices, and put into a small bowl to cool. Return the juices to the pan and cook over medium heat until reduced and slightly thickened.

To assemble the cake, put one cake layer on a serving plate or cake board. Spread one third of the frosting evenly across the top of the cake and top with just under a third of the apples and a third of the reduced apple caramel. Repeat with a second and third layer using the slightly larger portion of apple for the top layer. Serve immediately after assembling.

RED VELVET CAKE

This is one of my all-time favourite cakes, as it's moist, impressive to look at and, of course, absolutely delicious. Although it's not clear where the recipe originated, it has been around for decades and is very popular in the US and Canada. During the Second World War cocoa and food colouring were hard to come by so beetroot was often used instead to add colour. Many other recipes out there are a little restrained with the cocoa, but I think it should be an obvious flavour so I have increased the amount called for and dissolved it in water to help increase its flavour.

SERVES 12–16

225G UNSALTED BUTTER, AT ROOM
    TEMPERATURE, PLUS EXTRA FOR
    GREASING
350G PLAIN FLOUR, PLUS
    EXTRA FOR DUSTING
3 TABLESPOONS BOILING WATER
1 TEASPOON RED GEL FOOD
    COLOURING
40G COCOA POWDER
250ML BUTTERMILK
1 TEASPOON BICARBONATE OF SODA
¼ TEASPOON SALT
350G SUGAR
3 EGGS, LIGHTLY BEATEN
1 TEASPOON VANILLA EXTRACT
1 TABLESPOON WHITE VINEGAR

FOR THE CREAM CHEESE FROSTING
250G UNSALTED BUTTER, AT ROOM
    TEMPERATURE
500G ICING SUGAR
400G CREAM CHEESE (FULL FAT)
1 TEASPOON VANILLA EXTRACT

Preheat the oven to 170°C (150°C fan oven) gas mark 3. Lightly grease three 20cm round cake tins and line the bases with baking parchment, then grease these too. Dust with flour and tap out any excess. In a small bowl mix together the boiling water, food colouring, cocoa powder and buttermilk until fully combined, set aside.

Sift the flour, bicarbonate of soda and salt into a medium bowl. Using an electric mixer, beat the butter and sugar until light and fluffy, about 5 minutes.

Beat in the eggs, a little at a time, until fully combined, then mix in the vanilla extract. Turn the mixer to low and add a third of the flour mixture followed by half the buttermilk mixture. Repeat and then add the final third of flour mixture. Stir in the vinegar.

Divide among the cake tins and bake for 25–30 minutes or until a cocktail stick inserted into the centre comes out clean. Allow to cool in the tins for 10 minutes before inverting onto wire racks to cool completely.

For the frosting, use an electric mixer to beat the butter until light and smooth, about 5 minutes. Slowly beat in the icing sugar until combined, then increase the speed and beat until light and fluffy. Beat in the cream cheese until just combined. Do not over-beat at this stage or the frosting will be too thin.

To assemble the cake, put a layer of cake on a serving plate or cake board. Spread a layer of frosting onto the top of the cake and put the second cake layer on top, then repeat. Put the final layer of cake on top and spread the remaining frosting over the top and sides of the cake.

ORANGE AND PASSION FRUIT CAKE

Everyone loves a classic lemon cake, but sometimes you want something a little different and for me this has just that twist. This moist and not-too-sweet orange loaf cake has a fresh and fragrant passion-fruit glaze, and is perfect with a cup of tea in the afternoon. If you want to freeze the cake, allow the unglazed cake to cool, then wrap it in two layers of clingfilm and a layer of foil. Add the glaze after it has thawed.

SERVES 10

225G UNSALTED BUTTER, AT ROOM TEMPERATURE, PLUS EXTRA FOR GREASING

225G PLAIN FLOUR

2 TEASPOONS BAKING POWDER

PINCH OF SALT

255G CASTER SUGAR

ZEST OF 2 LARGE ORANGES

4 LARGE EGGS, LIGHTLY BEATEN

JUICE OF 1 ORANGE

FOR THE PASSION FRUIT GLAZE

3 PASSION FRUITS

125G ICING SUGAR

Preheat the oven to 180°C (160°C fan oven) gas mark 4. Butter a 23 × 10cm loaf tin and line with a strip of baking parchment leaving about 2.5cm or so to hang over the edges, to make removing the cake easier. Sift the flour, baking powder and salt into a bowl, and set aside.

Using an electric mixer beat the butter, 225g of the sugar and the zest until light and fluffy, about 5 minutes. Beat in the eggs and 3 tablespoons orange juice, a little at a time, until fully incorporated.

Using a spatula, fold in the flour mixture. Scrape into the prepared tin, then level the top. Bake for 50–55 minutes or until risen and golden, and a cocktail stick inserted into the centre comes out clean.

While the cake is baking, make the syrup by putting the remaining orange juice and sugar into a small pan and simmering for a few minutes or until the sugar has dissolved.

Make holes all over the cake using a cocktail stick or skewer and brush with the orange syrup, allowing it to soak into the cake. Leave to cool in the tin for 10 minutes, then turn out onto a wire rack to cool completely.

To make the glaze, scoop out the seeds and pulp from the passion fruits and press through a sieve, retaining about 1 tablespoon of the seeds. Mix the juice, icing sugar and reserved seeds together until thick and smooth, then pour over the cake, letting it drip down the sides.

TIP
If you don't like passion fruit you could use chocolate glaze (page 32) instead.

CHAI TEA AND MILK CHOCOLATE CUPCAKES

Cupcakes shot to popularity a number of years ago and, despite many opinions to the contrary, they don't seem to be going anywhere soon. Rather than ignore them completely, I thought I would make some that are more suited to my taste, so these ones are not just a plain vanilla sponge but moist and flavourful instead. As with all cakes, overmixing is the enemy, it will make your cakes dry and tough, so only mix in the flour until it is just fully combined.

MAKES 12

1 TABLESPOON CHAI TEA
(FROM ABOUT 3 TEA BAGS)
225G PLAIN FLOUR
2 TEASPOONS BAKING POWDER
225G BUTTER, AT ROOM
TEMPERATURE
225G CASTER SUGAR
4 EGGS, LIGHTLY BEATEN
125ML SOURED CREAM
GRATED OR MELTED CHOCOLATE,
TO DECORATE (OPTIONAL)

FOR THE FROSTING
200G GOOD-QUALITY MILK
CHOCOLATE
225G BUTTER, AT ROOM
TEMPERATURE
1 TABLESPOON MILK
½ TEASPOON VANILLA EXTRACT
225G ICING SUGAR

Preheat the oven to 180°C (160°C fan oven) gas mark 4. Line a standard 12-cup muffin pan with paper cases. If the tea isn't already fine, you may need to grind it using a pestle and mortar. Sift the flour, baking powder and chai tea into a medium bowl, then set aside.

Using an electric mixer, beat the butter and sugar until light and fluffy, about 5 minutes. Beat in the eggs, a little at a time, beating until fully combined, then add a third of the flour mixture followed by half the soured cream. Repeat and then add the final third of flour mixture.

Divide the batter equally among the paper cases and bake for 20–25 minutes or until a cocktail stick inserted into the centre of one of the cakes comes out clean. Transfer to a wire rack to cool completely.

To make the frosting, melt the chocolate in a microwave or a heatproof bowl over a pan of gently simmering water, making sure the base of the bowl doesn't touch the water. Once melted, remove from the heat and allow to cool to room temperature.

Using an electric mixer, beat the butter until smooth and creamy, about 3 minutes. Slowly incorporate the melted chocolate, milk and vanilla, mixing until smooth. Add the icing sugar a little at a time, beating until fully combined.

Spread the frosting onto the cooled cupcakes using a small offset spatula or a knife. Alternatively, use a piping bag fitted with a large star piping tube and pipe circles of frosting onto the cupcakes. If you wish, decorate with grated chocolate or a drizzle of melted chocolate.

MINI LEMON CAKES

These elegant little cakes have a full-on lemon flavour. With lemon zest in the batter, lemon syrup soaked into the cake and then a lemon glaze, the only way you could get more flavour into these cakes would be to add a filling of lemon curd, which of course you could do if you wanted. One of the wonderful things about this recipe is that the cakes keep really well for days, because the ground almonds and lemon syrup make them very moist.

MAKES 12

225G UNSALTED BUTTER, AT ROOM
  TEMPERATURE, PLUS EXTRA FOR
  GREASING
225G CASTER SUGAR
ZEST OF 2 LEMONS
125G FLOUR
100G GROUND ALMONDS
4 EGGS, LIGHTLY BEATEN
1 TEASPOON LEMON EXTRACT
  (OPTIONAL)

FOR THE LEMON SYRUP
JUICE OF 2 LEMONS
30G SUGAR

FOR THE LEMON GLAZE
JUICE OF ½ LEMON
100G ICING SUGAR

Preheat the oven to 180°C (160°C fan oven) gas mark 4 and lightly grease a 12-cup muffin pan, then set aside. Using an electric mixer, beat the butter, sugar and lemon zest until light and fluffy, about 5 minutes. Sift the flour and almonds into a medium bowl and set aside.

Add the eggs and lemon extract, if using, to the creamed mixture a little at a time, beating until fully combined. In two additions add the flour mixture and mix until just combined. Divide equally among the muffin cups and bake for 20–25 minutes or until golden around the edges and a cocktail stick inserted into the centre comes out clean.

While the cakes are baking, make the syrup. Add the lemon juice and sugar to a small pan set over medium heat and simmer for a few minutes or until the sugar has dissolved. Remove from the heat and set aside until needed.

Once the cakes are baked, remove them from the oven and allow them to cool for a few minutes. Using a cocktail stick or skewer, prick the cakes all over, then brush the cakes with the lemon syrup. Allow to cool in the pan for another 5 minutes before turning out onto a wire rack to cool completely. If the cakes have a pointed dome on top you can cut these off to create a more level surface.

To make the glaze, mix the lemon juice and icing sugar together until smooth. Turn the cakes upside down and spoon the glaze over, allowing it to drip slightly down the sides.

TIRAMISU CUPCAKES

If you are not a traditional cupcake fan, these are for you. They are very far from your standard cute cupcake; they are tiramisu recreated as cake. Although the recipe may appear to have quite a few stages, they are all easy, don't take long to complete and are really worth trying.

MAKES 12

225G PLAIN FLOUR

2 TEASPOONS BAKING POWDER

225G BUTTER, AT ROOM
  TEMPERATURE

225G CASTER SUGAR

4 EGGS, LIGHTLY BEATEN

125ML MILK

FOR THE COFFEE SYRUP

60ML FRESH ESPRESSO OR
  STRONG COFFEE

2 TEASPOONS CASTER SUGAR

1 TABLESPOON MARSALA (OPTIONAL)

FOR THE GANACHE

60ML DOUBLE CREAM

55G DARK CHOCOLATE (AT LEAST
  60–70% COCOA SOLIDS), BROKEN
  INTO PIECES

10G UNSALTED BUTTER

FOR THE FROSTING

250G MASCARPONE, AT ROOM
  TEMPERATURE

250ML DOUBLE CREAM

50G ICING SUGAR

Preheat the oven to 180°C (160°C fan oven) gas mark 4. Line a 12-cup muffin pan with paper cases. Sift the flour and baking powder into a medium bowl.

Using an electric mixer, beat the butter and sugar until light and fluffy, about 5 minutes. Beat in the eggs, a little at a time, beating until fully combined, then add a third of the flour mixture followed by half the milk. Repeat and then add the final third of flour mixture.

Divide equally among the paper cases and bake for 20–25 minutes or until a cocktail stick inserted into the centre of one of the cakes comes out clean. Just before the cupcakes are finished baking make the coffee syrup.

In a small bowl mix together the hot coffee, sugar and Marsala, if using. When the cupcakes are baked, remove from the oven and allow to cool for a few minutes, then prick the cakes all over with a cocktail stick or skewer. Brush liberally with the coffee syrup, then allow the cakes to cool completely.

To make the ganache, microwave the cream in a small bowl or a pan over a low heat until just at the boil, then add the chocolate and stir to combine. Once smooth and shiny, add the butter and mix together gently until combined.

To make the frosting, lightly beat the mascarpone until smooth. In a medium bowl whisk the cream until it holds medium-stiff peaks. Add a large spoonful of the cream to the mascarpone and mix to lighten, and then gently fold in the remaining cream and the icing sugar.

To assemble the cakes, cut a small piece of cake from the top of each cupcake, using a small sharp knife or an apple corer, and fill with the ganache. Using a small knife or offset spatula, spread the mascarpone frosting onto the cakes.

TIP
Because the frosting is made with cream, these cakes are best served the same day they are made.

PISTACHIO AND RASPBERRY FINANCIERS

Classically, these small French delicacies are made with ground almonds and served plain. They get their name from their traditional shape, a gold bar, and the fact that they originated in the financial district of Paris. My versions are still delicious little bites, but alongside almonds I have also used pistachio nuts and added raspberries for a more intense and interesting flavour. Browning the butter really adds to the warm, nutty flavour. Financiers are best served the day they are made.

MAKES 12

120G BUTTER, PLUS EXTRA FOR
   GREASING
100G PISTACHIO NUTS
120G ICING SUGAR
50G GROUND ALMONDS
50G FLOUR
PINCH OF SALT
4 EGG WHITES, LIGHTLY BEATEN
1 TEASPOON VANILLA EXTRACT
24 RASPBERRIES
ICING SUGAR, TO SERVE

Preheat the oven to 180°C (160°C fan oven) gas mark 4 and lightly grease a 12-cup muffin pan. Put the butter in a medium pan set over medium heat and cook, swirling the pan occasionally, until the butter turns a medium brown. Remove from the heat and pass through a fine sieve into a small bowl.

Put the pistachio nuts and icing sugar into the bowl of a food processor and process until finely ground. In a medium bowl mix together the pistachio nut mixture, almonds, flour and salt.

Add the egg whites and vanilla, and mix together, making sure everything is evenly combined. Mix in the warm browned butter a little at a time until combined.

Divide the financier batter evenly between the muffin cups and top each with two raspberries, pushing them in slightly.

Bake for 12–15 minutes or until the financiers are springy to the touch and lightly browned around the edges. Cool in the tin for 5 minutes, then turn out onto a wire rack to cool completely. Dust with icing sugar to serve, if you wish.

GIANDUJA DACQUOISE CAKE

This a perfect dinner-party dessert, as it is mostly prepared ahead of time. Using Italian inspirations of gelato and gianduja (a hazelnut and chocolate confection from Turin) as my starting point, I came up with my take on an ice cream cake: layers of nutty meringue sandwiched together with ice cream and coated with an indulgent chocolate glaze – it will go down a treat.

SERVES 12

3 LARGE EGG WHITES
150G CASTER SUGAR
125G HAZELNUTS, FINELY CHOPPED
350G VANILLA ICE CREAM (PAGE 154)
   OR CHOCOLATE ICE CREAM,
   SOFTENED
100G PLAIN CHOCOLATE (AT LEAST
   60–70% COCOA SOLIDS)
140ML DOUBLE CREAM

Preheat the oven to 110°C (90°C fan oven) gas mark ¼. Line two baking trays with baking parchment and use a 23cm round cake tin as a template to draw a circle on each tray of baking parchment. Invert the paper so that the marks are on the underside.

To make the dacquoise, put the egg whites into a clean, grease-free bowl and whisk until they form soft peaks. With the mixer still on high, slowly pour in the sugar and continue to beat until the meringue holds stiff and glossy peaks.

Gently fold in 100g of the hazelnuts. Fill a piping bag, fitted with a large plain nozzle, with the dacquoise mixture and pipe a spiral onto each parchment tray starting at the centre of the template and finishing just within the line.

Bake for 2 hours or until the meringues are pale and crisp. Remove from the oven and place the meringues onto wire racks to cool completely.

To assemble the cake, put one of the meringues into a cake tin and spread the softened ice cream in an even layer, reaching all the way to the edges. Top with the second meringue and gently press into the ice cream. Wrap the cake tin with clingfilm and freeze for 2 hours or until the ice cream is firm.

To serve, remove the cake from the freezer while you make the glaze. Put the chocolate into a medium bowl and the cream in a small pan set over medium heat. Bring the cream just to the boil, remove from the heat and pour over the chocolate, then stir to combine.

Invert the cake onto a serving plate and pour the glaze over the cake. Spread lightly to allow the glaze to drip down the sides. Sprinkle the cake with the remaining hazelnuts and serve immediately.

PEACHES-AND-CREAM UPSIDE-DOWN CAKE

This is a perfect cake for a summer's afternoon, as the peach makes it look fresh and bright, but it also feels a little indulgent because of the caramel topping. My favourite way to enjoy it is with a drizzle of cream, but it would be equally delicious with a scoop of homemade vanilla ice cream (page 154).

SERVES 8–10

115G BUTTER, PLUS EXTRA FOR
   GREASING
210G FLOUR
2 TEASPOONS BAKING POWDER
PINCH OF SALT
200G CASTER SUGAR
ZEST OF 1 ORANGE
2 LARGE EGGS, LIGHTLY BEATEN
1 TEASPOON VANILLA EXTRACT
120ML SOURED CREAM

FOR THE TOPPING
10G BUTTER
35G LIGHT BROWN SUGAR
3 PEACHES, PEELED

Preheat the oven to 180°C (160°C fan oven) gas mark 4 and lightly grease a deep 20cm diameter round cake tin and line with baking parchment. Sift the flour, baking powder and salt together into a medium bowl and set aside.

Using an electric mixer, beat the butter, sugar and orange zest together until light and fluffy, about 5 minutes. Beat in the eggs and vanilla, a little at a time, beating until fully combined.

Add a third of the flour mixture followed by half the soured cream. Repeat and then add the final third of flour mixture, beating until just combined.

To make the topping, melt the butter and brown sugar together in a small pan and pour evenly across the base of the prepared tin. Slice the peaches in half, remove the stone and cut each half into four slices. Spread across the base of the prepared tin and top with the cake batter in an even layer. Bake in the preheated oven for 50–55 minutes or until a cocktail stick inserted into the centre comes out clean. Cool in the tin for 5 minutes, then turn out onto a wire rack to cool a little. Best served warm. Cut into slices to serve.

TIP
You can make this cake with all sorts of fruit, from apple to pineapple. Make the recipe yours.

FAMILY CHRISTMAS CAKE

I have no idea how old this recipe is; it has definitely been made every Christmas by my mum and before that by my nanna, so who knows how old it really is? When I was taught this recipe there wasn't even anything written down, it was one of those recipes that just existed in family members' heads. This cake is a little different from the traditional dark and heavy cakes that so many people don't like, it is lighter and less dense.

SERVES 15–20

225G SULTANAS
225G RAISINS
225G CURRANTS
110G MIXED CANDIED PEEL
110G GLACÉ CHERRIES
ZEST OF 1 LEMON
ZEST OF 1 ORANGE
4 TABLESPOONS BRANDY
225G BUTTER, AT ROOM
    TEMPERATURE, PLUS EXTRA
    FOR GREASING
225G PLAIN FLOUR
110G GROUND ALMONDS
¼ TEASPOON SALT
1½ TEASPOONS GROUND CINNAMON
1½ TEASPOONS MIXED SPICE
225G CASTER SUGAR
5 LARGE EGGS, LIGHTLY BEATEN

The night before you want to make the cake, put the fruits, zests and brandy into a large bowl and mix together. Cover with clingfilm and leave to soak overnight.

The following day preheat the oven to 150°C (130°C fan oven) gas mark 2. Grease and triple line with parchment an 8cm deep, 25cm round cake tin. Sift the flour, almonds, salt and spices together into a medium bowl.

Put the butter and sugar into a large bowl and, using an electric mixer, beat until light and fluffy, about 5 minutes. Beat in the eggs a little at a time, beating until fully combined.

With the mixer on low, add the flour mixture, a large spoonful at a time, mixing until just combined. Using a spatula or metal spoon, fold in the soaked fruit.

Scrape the batter into the prepared pan and bake for 1 hour. Reduce the temperature to 110°C (90°C fan oven) gas mark ¼ and bake for a further 2 hours or until a cocktail stick inserted into the centre comes out clean. If the cake is browning too fast, cover the top lightly with a tent of foil. Allow the cake to cool completely in the tin before removing.

MINCEMEAT SCONES

Scones are definitely a childhood favourite of mine. They were one of the first things I was taught to bake and something I fondly remember having on family holidays in Devon. This is my mum's recipe and, rather than keeping them classic and plain or simply with raisins, my mum had the amazing idea to add mincemeat. The spicy syrup surrounding the fruit gives the scones a gentle, warm flavour that I adore.

MAKES 12

340G SELF-RAISING FLOUR
1 TEASPOON BAKING POWDER
40G CASTER SUGAR
85G UNSALTED BUTTER,
   IN SMALL PIECES
85ML WHOLE MILK
2 EGGS
60G MINCEMEAT

Preheat the oven to 190°C (170°C fan oven) gas mark 5 and line a baking tray with baking parchment. Sift the flour and baking powder into a large bowl and stir in the sugar. Add the butter and rub into the flour until the mixture resembles fine breadcrumbs.

Pour the milk into a jug and add 1 egg and the mincemeat. Mix together. Make a well in the flour mixture and pour in the liquid, then bring it together with your hands. As the mixture begins to hold together, tip it onto the work surface and gently knead ten or twelve times, making sure not to rip or stretch the dough, just until the dough forms a smooth ball.

Lightly press the dough into a circle, 2.5cm thick. Use a floured 6cm round cutter and cut out as many scones as you can. Don't twist the cutter as you press it into the dough, as this will affect the rise. Lightly knead the scraps together and cut out the remaining scones.

Beat the remaining egg and use to glaze the tops of the scones. Bake for 15–20 minutes or until the scones are golden and risen. Remove from the oven and allow them to cool on a wire rack before serving.

NANNA'S GINGERBREAD

This is my nanna's original recipe for gingerbread with no alterations, no tweaks, nothing, just her classic recipe, which means it is at least over 60 years old. When I was looking through my family recipes and found my nanna's original handwritten recipe, I had to do some research, as it was so old that the units of measurement were no longer used. The milk was measured in gills, for example! But that at least makes me feel that the recipe has stood the test of time.

SERVES 16

170G BUTTER, PLUS EXTRA FOR
    GREASING

115G CASTER SUGAR

20G ORANGE MARMALADE

350G GOLDEN SYRUP

2 EGGS

210ML MILK

2 TABLESPOONS STEM GINGER,
    CHOPPED

340G PLAIN FLOUR

3 TEASPOONS GROUND GINGER

1 TEASPOON ALLSPICE

1 TEASPOON CINNAMON

1 TEASPOON BICARBONATE OF SODA

PINCH OF SALT

PINCH OF CAYENNE PEPPER

Preheat the oven to 150°C (130°C fan oven) gas mark 2 and lightly grease a 20cm square cake tin. Line with baking parchment paper, leaving about a 5cm overhang, making it easier to remove the cake later. Melt the butter, sugar, marmalade and syrup together in a medium pan over medium heat. Set the pan aside to cool. In a separate bowl whisk the eggs and milk together.

Pour the butter mixture into the eggs and milk and add the stem ginger. Whisk together. Sift all the dry ingredients over the liquid mixture and gently fold together. Pour into the prepared tin and bake for 1–1¼ hours or until a cocktail stick inserted into the centre comes out clean. Cool in the tin for 5 minutes, then turn out onto a wire rack to cool completely. Cut into squares to serve.

TIP
The texture and flavour of this cake improves overnight.

GUINNESS PARKIN

My older sister and brother say that the sign of a good nanna is having a tin full of parkin in the house at all times. In fact as a unique way of announcing that she was pregnant, my sister presented her mum with a batch of parkin and let her figure out for herself that she was about to become a nanna! This version of nanna's recipe has been played around with a little and has had Guinness added, which gives the cake a huge amount of depth and warmth, adding hugely to the ginger flavour. Like many gingerbreads, the flavour and texture gets better with a few days' keeping. It will lasts at least four or five days without drying out.

MAKES 10

110G BUTTER, MELTED AND
    COOLED, PLUS EXTRA FOR
    GREASING
250G PLAIN FLOUR
2 TEASPOONS BAKING POWDER
3 TABLESPOONS GROUND GINGER
1 TEASPOON GROUND CINNAMON
¼ TEASPOON GROUND CLOVES
225G BLACK TREACLE
125ML GUINNESS (YOU CAN USE MILK
    FOR A NON-ALCOHOLIC
    ALTERNATIVE)
¼ TEASPOON BICARBONATE OF SODA
2 EGGS, LIGHTLY BEATEN
200G CASTER SUGAR

Preheat the oven to 180°C (160°C fan oven) gas mark 4. Grease a 23 × 10cm loaf tin and line with baking parchment, leaving a roughly 5cm overhang so that you can remove the cake more easily later. Sift the flour, baking powder, ginger, cinnamon and cloves together into a medium bowl and set aside.

Put the treacle and Guinness into a medium pan and bring to the boil. Turn off the heat and add the bicarbonate of soda. The mixture will bubble and foam; set aside until it settles down.

In a medium bowl, whisk the eggs and sugar together until thickened and pale. Drizzle in the butter and whisk to combine. Then whisk the Guinness mixture into the eggs.

Sift the flour mixture over the liquid ingredients and gently fold together until combined. Pour into the prepared tin and bake for 1 hour or until a cocktail stick inserted into the centre comes out clean.

Remove from the oven and allow to cool in the tin for 10 minutes before inverting onto a wire rack to cool completely.

CHOCOLATE AND CHESTNUT TORTE

This is a surprisingly light chocolate cake — it looks decadent and rich but it's actually melt-on-the-tongue light. Basically a cooked mousse, it has no flour but the subtle addition of chestnut adds a real depth to the cake. I prefer to serve this slightly warm with chestnut cream, but it can also be served chilled straight from the fridge.

SERVES 18

150G UNSALTED BUTTER, PLUS EXTRA
    FOR GREASING
200G DARK CHOCOLATE (AT LEAST
    60–70% COCOA SOLIDS)
100G SWEETENED CHESTNUT PURÉE
100G LIGHT BROWN SUGAR
4 EGGS, SEPARATED
50G CASTER SUGAR

FOR THE CHESTNUT CREAM
240ML DOUBLE CREAM
100G SWEETENED CHESTNUT PURÉE

Preheat the oven to 180°C (160°C fan oven) gas mark 4. Line the base of a 23cm springform cake tin with baking parchment, lightly greasing the sides.

Set a heatproof bowl over a pan of lightly simmering water, making sure the bowl doesn't touch the water. Add the chocolate and butter and allow to melt, stirring occasionally.

In a medium bowl, whisk together the chestnut purée, light brown sugar and egg yolks until thickened and pale.

Put the egg whites into a clean, grease-free bowl (this is best done using a freestanding electric mixer) and whisk until they form soft peaks, then slowly pour in the caster sugar and whisk until the meringue is stiff and shiny.

Whisk the melted chocolate into the chestnut mixture, then mix in one third of the meringue. Gently fold in the remaining meringue, trying to knock out as little air as possible.

Pour the batter into the prepared tin and level gently. Bake in the preheated oven for 35–40 minutes or until the cake is risen and has a thin, cracked top. Leave to cool for 10 minutes before removing the springform side, then allow to cool completely.

To make the chestnut cream, put the cream and chestnut purée into a bowl and whisk to combine. If you like a pouring consistency, serve it this way, but if you prefer it to be thicker, continue whisking until the cream holds soft peaks.

REDCURRANT CHEESECAKE

This is an adaptation of a family recipe that is at least 40 years old. It was sent to my mum from Australia via telegram and appears at the end of a long letter from family members who had emigrated. Cheesecake obviously wasn't well known at the time, because our relative wrote to reassure us: 'it isn't half as yucky as it sounds'! I have added the fruit and increased the volume of the recipe, to make a taller and more impressive end result. The key to a creamy cheesecake is to bake it slowly and to just the right stage. It should still have a wobbly centre when it comes out of the oven, and needs to be chilled for at least eight hours before serving.

SERVES 12–16

225G DIGESTIVE OR RICH TEA
   BISCUITS
110G BUTTER, MELTED
900G FULL-FAT CREAM CHEESE
450G CASTER SUGAR
1 TABLESPOON FLOUR
4 EGGS, LIGHTLY BEATEN
1 TEASPOON VANILLA BEAN PASTE

FOR THE TOPPING
350G REDCURRANTS
150G CASTER SUGAR
ZEST OF 1 ORANGE
JUICE ½ ORANGE

Preheat the oven to 180°C (160°C fan oven) gas mark 4 and line the base of a 23cm springform cake tin with baking parchment. Put the biscuits into a food processor and pulse until they resemble breadcrumbs. (Alternatively, put them in a plastic bag and crush with a rolling pin.)

Put the biscuit crumbs in a bowl and pour in the melted butter. Mix well then press firmly into the base and a little up the sides of the prepared tin. Bake for 10 minutes, then reduce the temperature to 150°C (130°C fan oven) gas mark 2. Remove the tin from the oven and set aside.

Using an electric mixer, beat the cream cheese until smooth and creamy, about 3 minutes. Add the sugar and flour, and beat until combined.

Beat in the eggs and vanilla, a little at a time, beating until just fully combined. Pour onto the baked base and level out with a spatula. Bake for 1½ hours or until set around the edges but still wobbly in the centre. Cool completely in the tin, then chill for 8 hours or until ready to serve.

To make the topping, put the fruit, sugar, zest and orange juice into a small pan. Bring to the boil over low heat and when the fruit starts to pop remove from the heat and allow to cool. Pour over the top of the cake to serve.

TIP
You can, of course, use any topping you want; it would be equally delicious with something like blueberries or peaches.

BARS
AND
COOKIES

FUDGE BROWNIES

If you're a bit of a chocoholic, then brownies are your ultimate fix – pure unadulterated chocolate, nothing else needed. Yes, you could add nuts or other flavourings, but a simple brownie really is a wonderful thing. If you want your brownies fudgy, be careful to only just fold in the flour until it can no longer be seen. If you prefer your brownies a little cakier, then beat in the flour for a few minutes, to develop the gluten so the brownies form a crust and rise a little.

MAKES 16

180G PLAIN FLOUR

3 TABLESPOONS COCOA POWDER

¼ TEASPOON SALT

300G DARK CHOCOLATE (AT LEAST 60–70% COCOA SOLIDS)

200G UNSALTED BUTTER

150G CASTER SUGAR

220G LIGHT BROWN SUGAR

4 EGGS

1 TEASPOON VANILLA EXTRACT

Preheat the oven to 180°C (160°C fan oven) gas mark 4. Grease a 23 × 33cm baking tin and line it with baking parchment, leaving a 5cm overhang along the long edges to make removing the brownies easier. Sift the flour, cocoa powder and salt together into a bowl and set aside.

In a medium pan set over medium heat melt the chocolate and butter together, whisk in the sugars, then remove from the heat. Firmly whisk in the eggs and vanilla until fully combined and the batter has slightly thickened.

Fold in the flour mixture until just combined – the odd speck of flour showing is fine. Pour the batter into the prepared tin and level the top with a spatula. Bake for 30 minutes or until a cocktail stick inserted into the centre comes out with just a few moist crumbs.

Allow to cool in the pan completely before removing and slicing into squares.

CHEWY SPECULAAS BLONDIES

I am in love with speculaas – I mean, what's not to love? The Belgian classic is like a gingerbread biscuit, warm and toasty from the spices but crunchy like a sugar biscuit – they are simply delicious. I thought it would a great idea to put the same flavours into a chewy blondie, and boy are these good! Blondies are similar to brownies, but as they are made with brown sugar, the flavour is reminiscent of butterscotch. When you take them out of the oven they need to cool completely before removing or cutting them, as they need a few hours to firm up. If you want to take these to the next level, break up some speculaas biscuits (either homemade or shop bought) into the batter before baking.

MAKES 16

225G UNSALTED BUTTER, PLUS EXTRA FOR GREASING
1 TEASPOON GROUND GINGER
¼ TEASPOON FRESHLY GRATED NUTMEG
¼ TEASPOON GROUND CLOVES
⅛ TEASPOON GROUND CARDAMOM PODS
400G LIGHT BROWN SUGAR
2 EGGS
250G PLAIN FLOUR
¼ TEASPOON SALT
1 TEASPOON BAKING POWDER
80G GOOD-QUALITY MILK CHOCOLATE, ROUGHLY CHOPPED (OR CHOCOLATE CHIPS)
80G HAZELNUTS, CHOPPED

Preheat the oven to 180°C (160°C fan oven) gas mark 4. Grease a 23 × 33cm baking tin and line with a strip of baking parchment, leaving a 5cm overhang along the long edges to make removing the blondies easier. Melt the butter in a pan over medium–high heat, add the spices and cook for a couple of minutes, then add the sugar and cook for a further 5 minutes, stirring constantly before taking the pan off the heat.

Leave to cool for 5 minutes, then whisk in the eggs and fold in the flour, salt and baking powder. Stir in the chocolate and hazelnuts, then pour the batter into the prepared tin and bake for 30 minutes. Allow to cool completely in the tin. Blondies take a few hours to firm up, so for ease leave in the tin overnight before cutting into squares.

PB+J
BARS

It may seem strange to some, but the combination of peanut butter and jam is totally delicious, so I've taken that American childhood favourite and used it to create an easy traybake using shortbread as its base. To ensure the shortbread keeps its shape when baking, chill it after handling; this will ensure that you don't warm up the butter, which would make for a poor base.

MAKES 12

450G FLOUR

150G CASTER SUGAR

300G UNSALTED BUTTER, CHILLED AND
  CUT INTO SMALL CUBES

PINCH OF SALT

150G PEANUT BUTTER

300G RASPBERRY JAM

Press a piece of foil into the base and up the sides of a 23 × 33cm baking tin. Put the flour, sugar, butter and salt into the bowl of a food processor and pulse until the mixture just starts to form into a dough. (Alternatively, add the butter into the flour, salt and sugar and rub in with the fingertips or using a pastry blender.) Turn out onto the work surface and knead together lightly until uniform.

Take about two thirds of the dough and press into the base of the prepared pan. Chill for 15 minutes. Wrap the other third of the mixture in clingfilm and chill. Preheat the oven to 180°C (160°C fan oven) gas mark 4.

Bake the shortbread base for 25–30 minutes or until lightly golden around the edges. Cool the baked base for 20 minutes.

Spread the peanut butter evenly over the cooled base, then spread over the jam. Crumble the leftover shortbread mixture and scatter evenly over the jam. Bake for a further 25–30 minutes or until the crumbled shortbread starts to colour. Allow to cool completely before cutting into squares.

NANAIMO BARS

This is a quintessentially Canadian recipe, hailing from the small town of Nanaimo in British Columbia. It was first created in the early 1950s by a Canadian housewife who submitted it to the annual Women's Institute fundraising cookbook. It quickly grew in popularity, and was recently voted 'Canada's Favourite Confection' in a newspaper survey. I tried them first in Nanaimo itself when on holiday visiting family in Vancouver, so they have a fond place in my heart, and my stomach. They are fairly rich, so instead of cutting into large squares, as you would a tray of brownies, cut them into more manageable squares. This recipe makes lots, so it's perfect for a big party, and there's no baking involved – it's a fridge cake – so it's very straighforward.

MAKES ABOUT 40

300G DIGESTIVE OR RICH TEA
   BISCUITS
170G BUTTER
75G CASTER SUGAR
45G COCOA POWDER
2 LARGE EGGS
1 TEASPOON VANILLA EXTRACT
100G DESICCATED COCONUT
75G WALNUTS, COARSELY CHOPPED

FOR THE MIDDLE LAYER
85G BUTTER
345G ICING SUGAR
3 TABLESPOONS CUSTARD POWDER
100ML DOUBLE CREAM

FOR THE TOP LAYER
225G DARK CHOCOLATE (AT LEAST
   60–70% COCOA SOLIDS), FINELY
   CHOPPED
200ML DOUBLE CREAM
40G UNSALTED BUTTER, SOFTENED

Press a piece of foil into the base and up the sides of a 23 × 33cm baking pan and set aside. Put the biscuits into a food processor and pulse until they resemble breadcrumbs. (Alternatively, put them in a plastic bag and crush with a rolling pin.) Set aside.

Melt the butter in a medium pan set over medium heat. Remove from the heat and whisk in the sugar and cocoa powder, then gradually beat in the eggs. Put back on the heat and cook, whisking constantly, until the mixture thickens, about 1 minute. Remove from the heat and stir in the vanilla, coconut, biscuit crumbs and walnuts. Press this mixture evenly into the prepared pan, making sure to press the mixture in firmly so that it isn't too crumbly when cut. Chill until firm, about 1 hour.

To make the middle layer, beat the butter using an electric mixer until light and fluffy, then gradually beat in the icing sugar until smooth. Add the custard powder and cream, and beat slowly until combined, then beat on high until light and fluffy. Spread in an even layer across the chilled base, then chill for a further 30 minutes.

To make the top layer, put the chocolate into a medium bowl and set aside. In a medium pan bring the cream just to the boil, then pour over the chocolate. Leave to stand for 2 minutes before gently stirring together until smooth. Add the butter and stir until the ganache is smooth. Pour over the custard layer and spread in an even layer. Chill until set. To serve use a sharp knife and cut into small squares.

TIP
To get a clean cut run the knife under hot water, then wipe dry, before cutting.

CHERRY
LINZER
SLICES

Another easy traybake, this one is a take on the Austrian dessert Linzer Torte, a recipe that can be traced as far back as 1653. It is a dough flavoured with hazelnuts, cinnamon and cloves, and filled with cherries. My version uses a spiced shortbread as the base and the topping, and is filled with cherry jam.

MAKES ABOUT 12

125G SUGAR

130G HAZELNUTS

300G PLAIN FLOUR

1 TEASPOON GROUND CINNAMON

¼ TEASPOON GROUND CLOVES

250G BUTTER, CHILLED AND CUT
  INTO SMALL CUBES

1 EGG, LIGHTLY BEATEN

350G CHERRY JAM

Press a piece of foil into the base and up the sides of a 23 × 33cm baking tin. In the bowl of a food processor pulse the sugar and hazelnuts until fine. Add the flour and spices, then pulse just to combine.

Add the butter and pulse until the mixture resembles coarse breadcrumbs. Add the egg and pulse just until the dough starts to come together. Turn out onto the work surface and knead together lightly until uniform.

Take about two thirds of the dough and press it into the base of the prepared tin. Wrap the remaining dough in clingfilm and chill. Chill the base for 15 minutes or until firm. Preheat the oven to 180°C (160°C fan oven) gas mark 4. Bake the base for 30–35 minutes or until lightly golden around the edges. Cool for 20 minutes.

Spread the jam evenly across the cooled base and set aside. Take the remaining chilled dough and roll it to about 3mm thick. Cut out strips of dough 1cm wide and lay them over the jam in a lattice pattern. Bake for a further 25–30 minutes or until the linzer dough starts to colour. Allow to cool completely in the tin before removing and cutting into slices, or use a cookie cutter to cut out shapes.

NUTELLA AND BANANA BITES

These are the ideal treat for a child's birthday party. Nutella, chocolate, bananas and marshmallow crispy treats are all childhood favourites, and they are so easy to make. There isn't even any baking as this is a super fast fridge cake. This recipe makes a 20cm square slab and I would suggest cutting it into small squares. It makes a lot, but they are rather addictive, so you may want to go back for a second piece.

MAKES ABOUT 20 SQUARES

VEGETABLE OIL, FOR GREASING

3 TABLESPOONS BUTTER

140G MINI MARSHMALLOWS

75G RICE KRISPIES

100G MILK CHOCOLATE, BROKEN
   INTO PIECES

275G NUTELLA

2 LARGE BANANAS

Press a piece of foil into the base and up the sides of a 20cm square baking tin and very lightly grease it with vegetable oil. Set aside.

Melt the butter in a large pan set over medium heat. Add the marshmallows and stir until melted and smooth. Immediately remove from the heat and add the Rice Krispies. Stir to coat evenly.

Using a large, lightly oiled spoon, press the crispy mixture firmly into an even layer in the prepared tin.

For the topping, melt the chocolate and Nutella in a microwave or a heatproof bowl over a pan of gently simmering water, making sure the base of the bowl doesn't touch the water. Once melted, remove from the heat and allow to cool slightly.

Meanwhile, slice the bananas thinly and spread in an even layer across the crispy base. Pour the Nutella mixture over the bananas and use an offset spatula to level it out. Put the tray in the fridge until set, then use a sharp knife to cut into squares.

ROSE AND RASPBERRY MACARONS

Macarons remind me of walking through the streets of Paris looking through the many patisserie windows trying to decide what to buy. Once you have learnt the technique there is no end to the flavour combinations you can try, but here I have used one of my all-time favourites. Rose is often thought of as an old-fashioned and soapy flavour, but if you use rose syrup rather than rose water and you are careful with the amount used, it is absolutely delicious.

MAKES ABOUT 30

170G ICING SUGAR

160G GROUND ALMONDS

120ML EGG WHITES FROM ABOUT 4
    MEDIUM EGGS, DIVIDED INTO TWO
    EQUAL BATCHES

160G GRANULATED SUGAR

1 TEASPOON RED POWDERED FOOD
    COLOURING

FOR THE ROSE BUTTERCREAM

100G SUGAR

3 EGG YOLKS

225G BUTTER, AT ROOM
    TEMPERATURE, CUT INTO
    SMALL PIECES

2 TABLESPOONS ROSE SYRUP,
    OR TO TASTE

75G RASPBERRY JAM

Preheat the oven to 170°C (150°C fan oven) gas mark 3 and line two baking trays with baking parchment. Put the icing sugar and ground almonds into the bowl of a food processor and pulse until fully combined. Sift this mixture into a large bowl, discarding any small particles that stay in the sieve.

Add the first batch of egg whites to the almond mixture, mix together to form a thick paste, then set aside.

(*) Put 50ml water and the granulated sugar in a small pan set over medium heat. Bring to the boil and have a sugar thermometer ready. Meanwhile, put the second batch of egg whites into a clean, grease-free bowl (this is best done using a freestanding electric mixer) and whisk them on medium.

Start whisking the whites on high speed when the syrup in the pan reaches about 110°C on the sugar thermometer. Cook the syrup until it registers 118°C. Pour the syrup slowly down the side of the bowl with the whites, avoiding the beaters.

Continue to whisk the meringue on high until the mixture has cooled slightly and the bowl is no longer hot to the touch but is still warm. Add the food colouring and whisk to combine.

Scrape the meringue onto the almond mixture and gently fold together. It is important at this stage not to overmix the batter. The batter should fall in a thick ribbon from the spatula, fading back into the batter within about 30 seconds. If it doesn't, fold a few more times.

Add the batter to a piping bag fitted with a 1cm wide plain piping nozzle. Pipe rounds about 2.5cm in diameter onto the prepared baking trays. Leave to rest for 30 minutes or until the macarons have developed a skin and are no longer sticky, then bake for 12 minutes. Immediately slide the parchment onto the

work surface and allow the macarons to cool for a few minutes before gently peeling them off the paper. (*)

To make the rose buttercream, put the sugar and 2 tablespoons water into a small pan set over medium heat and bring to the boil. Cook until the syrup reaches 120°C. As the syrup nears the desired temperature, whisk the eggs yolks in a clean bowl until pale and increased in volume. With the mixer still on high, carefully pour the syrup into the eggs, avoiding the beaters. Whisk on high speed until cooled. Beat in the butter a few pieces at a time until silky and smooth. Add the rose syrup and mix to combine.

Fill a piping bag fitted with a small piping nozzle with the buttercream and pipe around the outside edge of half the macarons. Fill the centre with jam and sandwich with another macaron. Chill overnight before serving, allowing the macarons to come to room temperature first.

VARIATION
If you use green food colouring for the shells you could make the filling with mint chocolate.

MINT CHOCOLATE GANACHE
Put 220g finely chopped dark chocolate (at least 60–70% cocoa solids) into a medium bowl and set aside. Put 240ml double cream into a small pan set over medium heat and bring just to the boil. Pour over the chocolate and allow it to stand for a few minutes before stirring gently to combine. Add 50g unsalted butter, at room temperature and in small pieces, and 2 teaspoons peppermint extract to the chocolate mixture and gently stir until just smooth and combined. Allow the filling to stand until thickened enough to hold its shape. Fill a piping bag, fitted with a small piping nozzle, with the ganache and pipe onto half the macarons. Sandwich with another macaron.

HAZELNUT AND CHOCOLATE MACARONS

Macarons are traditionally made with ground almonds, which pair well with a range of other ingredients. They can actually also be made with many different kinds of nuts, such as pistachio or hazelnut, the latter of which happens to be my favourite. It has a very strong flavour and works wonderfully with chocolate. Whilst the ingredients are a little different, much of the method is exactly the same as for Rose and Raspberry Macarons (page 60).

MAKES ABOUT 30

170G ICING SUGAR

60G GROUND ALMONDS

100G HAZELNUTS, ROASTED AND SKINNED (SEE TIP)

120ML EGG WHITES FROM ABOUT 4 MEDIUM EGGS, DIVIDED INTO TWO EQUAL BATCHES

160G GRANULATED SUGAR

1 TEASPOON BROWN POWDERED FOOD COLOURING

FOR THE FILLING

220G DARK CHOCOLATE (AT LEAST 60–70% COCOA SOLIDS), FINELY CHOPPED

240G DOUBLE CREAM

50G UNSALTED BUTTER, AT ROOM TEMPERATURE

200G HAZELNUTS, ROASTED AND SKINNED

Preheat the oven to 170°C (150°C fan oven) gas mark 3 and line two baking trays with baking parchment. Put the icing sugar, ground almonds and hazelnuts in the bowl of a food processor and pulse until the hazelnuts are very fine. Sift this mixture into a large bowl, discarding any small particles that stay in the sieve.

Add the first batch of egg whites to the almond mixture, mix together to form a thick paste, then set aside.

Now refer to the recipe for Rose and Raspberry Macarons (page 60). Follow the method between the two stars (*).

To make the filling, put the chocolate in a medium bowl and set aside. Put the cream in a pan and bring just to the boil. Pour over the chocolate and allow to stand for a few minutes before gently stirring to form a silky ganache. Once combined, add the butter and mix gently to combine.

To finish the macarons fill a piping bag fitted with a small piping nozzle with the ganache and pipe onto half the macarons. Add a little chopped hazelnut to each and sandwich together with a second macaron. Chill overnight before serving, allowing them to come to room temperature first.

Tip
To roast and skin hazelnuts, spread them over a baking tray. Toast under a hot grill until golden brown, turning frequently. Put the hazelnuts in a clean tea towel and rub off the skins.

THICK AND CHEWY CHOCOLATE CHIP COOKIES

Chocolate chip cookies must be a favourite of almost every kid around, probably most adults too, for that matter! But do you want chewy or crunchy, thick or thin? I like mine thick and chewy, so these are my ideal version, full of gooey, melty chocolate. When beating the butter and sugar, remember you're not making a cake, so don't beat until light and fluffy, just until smooth and fully combined. If you overbeat the mixture your cookies will end up cakey. Because chocolate is the main flavour, don't skimp on quality, use good chocolate and avoid chocolate chips, because they don't melt in the same way and the cookies won't be as gooey.

MAKES ABOUT 25

500G PLAIN FLOUR

1 TEASPOON BICARBONATE OF SODA

1 TEASPOON BAKING POWDER

1 TEASPOON SEA SALT

225G UNSALTED BUTTER, AT ROOM TEMPERATURE

220G CASTER SUGAR

220G LIGHT BROWN SUGAR

2 EGGS, LIGHTLY BEATEN

1 TEASPOON VANILLA EXTRACT

500G CHOCOLATE DISCS OR CHOPPED BAR (AT LEAST 60–70% COCOA SOLIDS) (NOT CHIPS)

Sift the flour, bicarbonate of soda, baking powder and salt together into a medium bowl.

Using an electric mixer, beat the butter and sugars together until smooth, about 3 minutes. Add the eggs a little at a time, beating until fully combined, then mix in the vanilla extract.

In three additions, beat in the flour mixture, mixing until just combined. Fold in the chocolate. Ideally, chill the dough overnight before baking.

Preheat the oven to 180°C (160°C fan oven) gas mark 4 and line two baking trays with baking parchment. Use your hands or an ice cream scoop to form balls of dough, about 60g per cookie.

Bake six per tray for 16–18 minutes or until golden around the edges. Allow to cool for a few minutes before transferring to a wire rack to cool completely.

fleas....
flea collar: soak
a string in oil
of pennyroyal
(an herb). Change
collar every 2 weeks.
also bunches of the
herb may be hung in
doghouse. A pillow of
camomile flowers
will drive them away.

...mosquitoes will
avoid the smell
...nyroyal. Rub
...your skin
...chets with
...a

...an open dish "...
...ra ants hate sea sand &
oyster shells. Small black ants hate sprigs of wormwood (herb).
insects & spiders all flee from a cotton wad
.... soaked in oil of pennyroyal. Fleas & mosquitoes
hate the taste of vitamin B1. Take it orally.

MILK CHOCOLATE AND HAZELNUT COOKIES

I love the combination of milk chocolate and hazelnut, it's a classic and it works wonderfully in this recipe. The ground hazelnuts help to keep the cookie chewy and add a huge amount of flavour. If you are feeling inventive you could even play around with the type of nut used; why not try this recipe with pecans?

MAKES ABOUT 25

350G PLAIN FLOUR

1 TEASPOON BICARBONATE OF SODA

1 TEASPOON BAKING POWDER

½ TEASPOON SEA SALT

220G CASTER SUGAR

130G BLANCHED HAZELNUTS

220G LIGHT BROWN SUGAR

225G UNSALTED BUTTER, AT ROOM
    TEMPERATURE

2 EGGS

1 TEASPOON VANILLA EXTRACT

300G GOOD-QUALITY MILK
    CHOCOLATE, ROUGHLY CHOPPED

Sift the flour, bicarbonate of soda, baking powder and salt into a medium bowl and set aside.

In the bowl of a food processor add the caster sugar and hazelnuts, and process until finely ground. Grinding the nuts with the sugar reduces the risk of turning the nuts into a paste.

Using an electrical hand mixer, beat the hazelnut mixture and butter until smooth. Add the eggs, one at time, and the vanilla, beating until just combined. In three batches add the flour mixture and mix until just combined. Stir in the chocolate. Chill the dough at for at least 4 hours or until firm. Preheat the oven to 180°C (160°C fan oven) gas mark 4 and line two baking trays with baking parchment.

Divide the dough into balls using your hands or an ice cream scoop. (At this stage the dough can be frozen for up to one month.) Bake six balls per baking tray for 15 minutes or until the edges are golden but the centres look a little undercooked.

Allow to cool on the baking trays for a couple of minutes before removing to cool completely on wire racks.

PEANUT BUTTER AND MILK CHOCOLATE COOKIES

As a child I absolutely loved peanut butter, though my twin brother hated the stuff. Even he, however, is a fan of these delicious cookies. Soft and chewy with the addition of milk chocolate and pretzels, they are a delight. Make sure not to overbake them, as they won't retain the soft chewy centre.

MAKES ABOUT 22

300G PLAIN FLOUR

1 TEASPOON BAKING POWDER

1 TEASPOON BICARBONATE OF SODA

225G UNSALTED BUTTER, AT ROOM TEMPERATURE

2 EGGS

240G CASTER SUGAR

220G LIGHT BROWN SUGAR

250G SMOOTH PEANUT BUTTER

100G GOOD-QUALITY MILK CHOCOLATE, ROUGHLY CHOPPED

40G SALTED PEANUTS

40G SMALL PRETZELS, ROUGHLY BROKEN UP

Line two baking trays with baking parchment. Sift the flour, baking powder and bicarbonate of soda into a medium bowl and set aside.

Using an electric mixer, cream the butter and sugars until smooth, about 3 minutes. Beat in the eggs, one at time, until fully combined. Beat in the peanut butter until fully combined.

Mix in the flour until just combined. Fold in the chocolate, peanuts and pretzels. Chill the dough for 30 minutes or until firm. Preheat the oven to 180°C (160°C fan oven) gas mark 4.

Divide the dough into balls using your hands or an ice cream scoop. Put six on each tray and bake for 16–18 minutes or until browned on the edges and just starting to colour on the tops.

Allow to cool on the baking trays for a couple of minutes before removing to cool completely on wire racks.

DOUBLE CHOCOLATE AND SOUR CHERRY COOKIES

If you like chocolate – and really who doesn't? – then you will love these. Gooey and packed full of chocolate, they are a chocoholic's dream. With sour cherries to complement and cut the sweetness just a little, they really are an indulgent treat. Unlike many cookies, the dough is soft and a little sticky, so using an ice cream scoop really makes shaping the cookie dough easier, otherwise you can just drop large spoonfuls of dough onto the baking trays.

MAKES ABOUT 22

350G DARK CHOCOLATE (AT LEAST
   60–70% COCOA SOLIDS)
100G BUTTER, AT ROOM
   TEMPERATURE
100G CASTER SUGAR
150G LIGHT BROWN SUGAR
2 LARGE EGGS
130G PLAIN FLOUR
50G COCOA POWDER
1 TEASPOON BICARBONATE OF SODA
¼ TEASPOON SALT
100G DRIED SOUR CHERRIES

Preheat the oven to 180°C (160°C fan oven) gas mark 4 and line two baking trays with baking parchment. Break up 200g chocolate and melt in a heatproof bowl over a pan of gently simmering water, making sure the base of the bowl doesn't touch the water. Set the bowl aside to cool slightly. Roughly chop the remaining chocolate.

Using an electric mixer, beat the butter and sugars until light and fluffy, about 5 minutes. Beat in the eggs one at a time until well combined.

Sift the flour, cocoa, bicarbonate of soda and salt together into a bowl and, in three additions, add to the butter and sugar mixture, beating until just combined. With the mixer on medium, slowly pour in the melted chocolate, mixing until combined.

Add the remaining chocolate and the cherries, and stir to combine. Using an ice cream scoop, form balls of dough and place six per baking tray. Bake for 13 minutes or until they have crisped up around the edges. Allow to cool for 5 minutes before removing to cool completely on wire racks.

MY OATMEAL AND RAISIN COOKIES

Inspired by a blueberries-and-cream cookie I tried on a visit to a New York bakery, I came home and immediately came up with my own twist. The bakery used milk powder to add creaminess, and glucose to add a chewy texture, additions that really added something to the cookies. The version I created was also inspired by that glass of milk often drunk with an oatmeal raisin cookie, but with this recipe the 'milk' is already in the cookie.

MAKES ABOUT 20

175G RAISINS

280G PLAIN FLOUR

⅛ TEASPOON BICARBONATE OF SODA

¼ TEASPOON BAKING POWDER

½ TEASPOON SALT

30G NON-FAT MILK POWDER

225G UNSALTED BUTTER, AT ROOM TEMPERATURE

125G GRANULATED SUGAR

135G LIGHT BROWN SUGAR

60ML LIQUID GLUCOSE

1 LARGE EGG

40G WHITE CHOCOLATE, CHOPPED

95G PORRIDGE OATS

Line two baking trays with baking parchment. Put the raisins into a small bowl and pour over enough boiling water to cover. Leave for 10 minutes to soak. Drain the excess water and set the raisins aside.

Sift the flour, bicarbonate of soda, baking powder, salt and milk powder into a medium bowl.

In another bowl and using an electric mixer, beat the butter, sugars and glucose together until smooth and combined, about 2–3 minutes. Beat in the egg until fully combined. Beat in the flour mixture until just combined, then fold in the raisins, chocolate and oats.

Using your hands or an ice cream scoop, form balls of dough and put six per baking tray. Chill for 15 minutes. Preheat the oven to 180°C (160°C fan oven) gas mark 4. Bake the cookies for about 15 minutes or until the edges are golden. Cool on the tray for a couple of minutes before removing to wire racks to cool completely.

PASSION FRUIT SANDWICH BISCUITS

Here is my version of a Jammie Dodger, the childhood birthday-party favourite. Rather than using jam as the filling, I have used a passion fruit curd, which is bright and zingy. For the biscuits, I have added coconut which, although subtle, adds another layer of flavour. Once you have rolled and cut out the biscuits, chill them for 15 minutes or until firm, this will ensure they have nice clean edges when cooked.

MAKES ABOUT 15

325G PLAIN FLOUR, PLUS EXTRA
    FOR DUSTING
50G UNSWEETENED DESICCATED
    COCONUT
¼ TEASPOON SALT
200G SUGAR
225G BUTTER
1 EGG
1 YOLK
½ TEASPOON VANILLA EXTRACT
½ TEASPOON COCONUT EXTRACT

FOR THE PASSION FRUIT CURD

70ML PASSION FRUIT JUICE, ABOUT
    5 PASSION FRUITS (SEEDS RESERVED)
JUICE OF ½ LEMON
ZEST OF ½ LEMON
175G CASTER SUGAR
5 LARGE EGG YOLKS
100G BUTTER, SOFTENED,
    CUT INTO PIECES

To make the passion fruit curd, put the fruit juices, zest and sugar into a medium pan and whisk in the egg yolks. Cook over low heat, stirring constantly until the mixture thickens and coats the back of a spoon.

Pour into a medium bowl and stir in the butter, a few pieces at a time. Pour into a jar and chill until needed.

Put the flour, coconut, salt and sugar into the bowl of a food processor and pulse to combine. Add the butter and pulse until the mixture resembles coarse breadcrumbs. (Alternatively, rub the butter into the dry ingredients using the fingertips or a pastry blender.) Add the egg, egg yolk, vanilla and coconut extracts and pulse, or stir, until the mixture just comes together.

Tip onto the work surface and gently knead together until uniform. Divide the dough in half, wrap in clingfilm and chill for about 1 hour. Line two baking trays with baking parchment.

On a lightly floured work surface and working with one half of the dough at a time, roll out to a thickness of 5mm. Cut out rounds 7cm in diameter. Using a 2cm round cutter, remove a hole from the centre of half the rounds. Lift the biscuits off the surface with a spatula and put onto the baking tray. Chill for 15–20 minutes. Preheat the oven to 180°C (160°C fan oven) gas mark 4.

Bake for 13–15 minutes or until the edges turn golden. Allow to cool on the trays for 10 minutes before transferring to a wire rack to cool completely.

To assemble the biscuits, take the full circles and, using either a piping bag fitted with a small round nozzle, or a spoon, add a thin layer of passion fruit curd, leaving a thin border. Top with a ring biscuit, gently pressing them together, and then add a few reserved passion fruit seeds.

SPECULAAS

A spicy biscuit with plenty of crunch, Speculaas are a Belgian speciality. Although they are a traditional food that was once made only for St Nicholas's Eve they are, thankfully, now available all year round and are also sold commercially around the world. My recipe may not be traditional but it definitely carries the flavour of the classic version.

MAKES 35

425G PLAIN FLOUR, PLUS EXTRA FOR
   DUSTING
¼ TEASPOON SALT
¼ TEASPOON BAKING POWDER
4 TEASPOONS GROUND CINNAMON
2 TEASPOONS GROUND GINGER
½ TEASPOONS GROUND CLOVES
1 TEASPOON FRESHLY GRATED NUTMEG
200G LIGHT BROWN SUGAR
225G BUTTER, SLIGHTLY CHILLED
1 EGG
1 EGG YOLK
½ TEASPOON VANILLA EXTRACT
CASTER SUGAR, FOR SPRINKLING

Line two baking trays with baking parchment. Put the flour, salt, baking powder, spices and sugar in the bowl of a food processor and pulse to combine. Add the butter and pulse until the mixture resembles coarse breadcrumbs. (Alternatively, rub the butter into the dry ingredients using your fingertips or a pastry blender.) Add the egg, egg yolk and vanilla extract and pulse, or stir, until the mixture just comes together.

Tip onto the work surface and gently knead together until uniform. Divide the dough in half, wrap in clingfilm and chill for about 1 hour.

Lightly flour the work surface and, working with one half of the dough at a time, roll out to a thickness of about 4mm. Using a 7cm cookie cutter, cut out as many shapes as you can. Lift the biscuits off the surface with a spatula and put them onto the baking trays, then chill for 15–20 minutes. Preheat the oven to 180°C (160°C fan oven) gas mark 4.

Sprinkle the speculaas with a little caster sugar and bake them for 13–15 minutes or until the edges turn golden. Allow to cool on the baking trays for a couple of minutes before transferring to a wire rack to cool completely.

CRANBERRY AND MACADAMIA SHORTBREAD

Shortbread is delicious, sure, but why not play around with it and make it your own. Just because it has stood the test of time doesn't mean you can't change it up a bit. I have added orange and cranberries for flavour, which helps to balance out the rich nature of shortbread, and macadamia nuts for texture. You can easily change this recipe by using another fruit or nut.

MAKES ABOUT 15

225G PLAIN FLOUR
75G CASTER SUGAR
150G UNSALTED BUTTER,
  CUBED AND CHILLED
PINCH OF SALT
50G CRANBERRIES
50G MACADAMIA NUTS
ZEST OF 1 ORANGE

Preheat the oven to 180°C (160°C fan oven) gas mark 4 and line a baking tray with baking parchment. Put the flour into the bowl of a food processor with the sugar, butter and salt, then process until it forms a smooth dough. Pulse in the cranberries, macadamia nuts and orange zest to just combine evenly. (Alternatively, rub the butter into the dry ingredients using your fingertips or a pastry blender. Chop the cranberries and macadamia nuts, then stir them into the mixture with the orange zest.)

Turn the dough onto a lightly floured work surface and press into an even layer, about 1cm thick. Using a 7cm round cookie cutter, cut out as many shortbread circles as possible, then lightly knead the off-cuts and cut out more.

Bake in the preheated oven for 20 minutes or until the edges have turned golden. Allow to cool for 5 minutes before removing to cool completely on a wire rack.

DOUGHNUTS

I'm not sure I could pass a stand selling freshly fried doughnuts and not buy one, because doughnuts are surely addictive. Warm, soft, fluffy dough filled with something delicious – just too good to pass by. Although these ones can be made without a deep-fryer, it is much harder to regulate the temperature so I wouldn't advise it.

MAKES ABOUT 10

350G PLAIN FLOUR, PLUS EXTRA
    FOR DUSTING
150G CASTER SUGAR
1 TABLESPOON BAKING POWDER
½ TEASPOON SALT
240ML BUTTERMILK
1 EGG
2 EGG YOLKS
50ML VEGETABLE OIL
2 TEASPOONS VANILLA EXTRACT
VEGETABLE OIL, FOR DEEP-FRYING
CASTER SUGAR OR ICING SUGAR,
    FOR DUSTING

In large bowl, sift together the flour, sugar, baking powder and salt. In a small bowl whisk together the buttermilk, egg, egg yolks, oil and vanilla extract.

Make a well in the dry ingredients and pour in the buttermilk mixture, mix together until evenly combined. The dough will be very sticky at this stage. Cover the bowl with clingflim and chill for 1 hour.

Dust the work surface liberally with flour and, using floured hands, scrape out the dough and pat or roll out 1cm thick. Using a floured 7.5cm round cookie cutter, cut out the doughnuts, discarding the scraps. To make ring doughnuts, use a smaller cutter to remove the centres.

In a deep-fryer, heat the oil to 190°C (a small cube of bread should brown in 20 seconds). Fry two or three doughnuts at a time for 1½ minutes per side until golden brown. Remove with a slotted spoon and put on kitchen paper to drain off the excess oil.

Roll the doughnuts in caster or icing sugar and serve warm or at room temperature on the day of making.

VARIATIONS
If you would like to add a filling, try vanilla-flavoured Pastry Cream (page 165) or Chocolate Pastry Cream (page 165), or for something a bit more zingy, use Lemon Curd (page 166).

CECCLES CAKES

My mum is from Lancashire and my dad is from Yorkshire, so this recipe, an idea given to me by the chocolatier, Paul A. Young, is perfectly apt. It blends elements of the traditional Yorkshire curd tart and Lancashire Eccles cakes into something I'm calling Ceccles Cakes: a flaky pastry filled with a spiced fruit-and-curd mixture.

MAKES 6

2 PINTS WHOLE MILK

2 TABLESPOONS VEGETARIAN RENNET

1 QUANTITY FLAKY PASTRY
   (PAGE 168) OR 1KG SHOP-BOUGHT
   PUFF PASTRY

FLOUR, FOR DUSTING

1 EGG, LIGHTLY BEATEN

CASTER SUGAR, FOR SPRINKLING

FOR THE FILLING

60G BUTTER

125G SOFT BROWN SUGAR

175G CURRANTS

½ TEASPOON FRESHLY GRATED
   NUTMEG

1 TEASPOON GROUND CINNAMON

½ TEASPOON GROUND MIXED SPICE

The night before you want to make the cakes, put the milk in a medium pan and set over medium heat, then bring to 37°C (luke warm). Remove from the heat and stir in the rennet, then set aside for 1 hour. Line a fine sieve with muslin set over a large bowl.

Break up the curds a little and pour into the prepared sieve. Leave to drain overnight. Discard the liquid and retain the curds left in the sieve.

To make the filling, melt the butter and sugar in a small pan over medium heat, then stir in the fruit and spices and allow to cool before using. Preheat the oven to 200°C (180°C fan oven) gas mark 6 and line a baking tray with baking parchment.

Roll out the chilled pastry on a floured work surface to about 2–3mm thick, and cut out six rounds about 20cm in diameter. Divide the curds among the pastry rounds, leaving a 5cm border all around the curds. Top with the fruit mixture and fold the pastry border up and over the filling. Use a little water to seal the pastry.

Turn the cakes seal side down and use a sharp knife to pierce vent holes on top of each one. Brush with the beaten egg and sprinkle with a thin layer of caster sugar, then bake for 25–30 minutes or until the pastry is golden. Cool on the baking tray for 5 minutes, then turn out onto a wire rack to cool completely.

PASTRY

BLUEBERRY CRUMB TART

This is a tart that showcases blueberries at their best – rather like apples in an apple pie. Although simple in appearance and straightforward to make, it is still elegant enough to serve to company. If, after you have added the crumb topping, it seems to be browning too fast in the oven, tent a piece of foil over the top to prevent burning.

SERVES 8

½ QUANTITY SWEET PASTRY
   (PAGE 170) OR 500G SHOP-BOUGHT
   SWEET SHORTCRUST PASTRY
BUTTER, FOR GREASING
FLOUR, FOR DUSTING

FOR THE CRUMB TOPPING
75G CASTER SUGAR
75G GROUND ALMONDS
75G PLAIN FLOUR
1 TEASPOON GROUND CINNAMON
75G UNSALTED BUTTER, AT ROOM
   TEMPERATURE

FOR THE FILLING
575G BLUEBERRIES
ZEST OF ½ LEMON
2 TABLESPOONS LEMON JUICE
65G CASTER SUGAR
3 TABLESPOONS CORNFLOUR

Lightly grease a 23cm tart tin. To make the crumb topping, mix the dry ingredients together, then rub in the butter using your fingertips or a pastry blender. Gather the dough together, wrap in clingfilm and chill.

Remove the chilled sweet pastry from the fridge and leave to rest for 10 minutes. Lightly flour the work surface and the rolling pin, and roll out the pastry until 3–4mm thick, then use to line the prepared tart tin, trimming off the excess. Chill for 15 minutes. Preheat the oven to 180°C (160°C fan oven) gas mark 4.

Line the tart tin with baking parchment and fill with a layer of baking beans or rice. Bake for 15 minutes. Remove the parchment and beans, then bake for a further 5 minutes, until the pastry is starting to colour.

In a medium bowl, mix together all the filling ingredients and tip into the part-baked tart. Bake for 15 minutes. Crumble the topping and sprinkle it over the tart, then bake for a further 20 minutes, until the topping is lightly browned. Allow to cool in the tin before serving.

CHERRY CUSTARD TART

When I was little I used to look forward to the special treat of going to the bakery. The classic custard tart was one of my regular choices. I loved its simplicity, especially with the traditional topping of nutmeg. For my version, I have made it a little differently, taking my influence from the French dish, *clafoutis*, and adding fruit to the custard, which results in a deceptively simple but elegant tart.

SERVES 8

BUTTER, FOR GREASING

½ QUANTITY SWEET PASTRY
   (PAGE 170) OR 500G SHOP-BOUGHT
   SWEET SHORTCRUST PASTRY

FLOUR, FOR DUSTING

6 EGG YOLKS

75G CASTER SUGAR

250ML WHIPPING CREAM

100ML MILK

150G CHERRIES, STONED

Lightly grease a 23cm fluted tart tin. Take the chilled pastry out of the fridge and leave it to rest for 10 minutes. Lightly flour the work surface and the rolling pin, and roll out the pastry until 3–4mm thick. Line the prepared tart tin with the pastry, trimming off any excess, then chill for 15 minutes. Preheat the oven to 200°C (180°C fan oven) gas mark 6.

Line the tart shell with a piece of baking parchment and fill with a layer of baking beans or rice. Bake for 15 minutes. Remove the parchment and beans, then bake for a further 5 minutes or until the pastry starts to turn golden around the edges. Reduce the oven temperature to 170°C (150°C fan oven) gas mark 3.

In a small bowl whisk the egg yolks, sugar, cream and milk together until fully combined. Pour into the partially baked pastry shell and scatter the cherries over the top. Bake for 25–30 minutes or until the custard is just set and a little wobbly in the centre. Allow to cool in the tin on a wire rack. Serve cold.

CHOCOLATE, PECAN AND SALTED CARAMEL TART

Salted caramel and chocolate are a match made in heaven – so decadent and delicious that this tart just cries out to be made. The pecans give it a more rounded and interesting flavour and make for a very impressive-looking tart. If you are pushed for time you can make the pastry and caramel filling days in advance, then bake and assemble when needed, making the whole process very easy indeed. For a tart as flavourful as possible, make sure that you cook the caramel to be fairly dark. Don't burn it, but if you don't cook it enough it will just taste sweet and not of caramel.

SERVES 8–10

½ QUANTITY SWEET PASTRY
(PAGE 170) OR 500G SHOP-BOUGHT
SWEET SHORTCRUST PASTRY
FLOUR, FOR DUSTING
BUTTER, FOR GREASING

FOR THE CARAMEL LAYER
150G GRANULATED SUGAR
⅛ TEASPOON SEA SALT
90G DOUBLE CREAM
10G UNSALTED BUTTER, AT ROOM
    TEMPERATURE, CUT INTO SMALL
    PIECES
30G CRÈME FRAÎCHE
150G TOASTED PECANS,
    COARSELY CHOPPED

FOR THE CHOCOLATE LAYER
185ML DOUBLE CREAM
45G LIGHT BROWN SUGAR
225G DARK CHOCOLATE (AT LEAST
    60–70% COCOA SOLIDS), FINELY
    CHOPPED
40G UNSALTED BUTTER, SOFTENED,
    CUT INTO SMALL PIECES

Remove the chilled pastry from the fridge and allow to rest for 10 minutes. Lightly flour the work surface and the rolling pin, and roll out the pastry to about 4mm thick. Lightly butter a 23cm tart tin and line with the pastry. Chill for 30 minutes. Preheat the oven to 180°C (160°C fan oven) gas mark 4.

Line the tart with baking parchment and fill with a layer of baking beans or rice. Bake for 15 minutes. Remove the parchment and beans and bake for a further 10–15 minutes or until the pastry has turned a light golden brown. Allow to cool before removing from the tin and assembling the tart.

To make the caramel layer, in a medium pan melt the sugar over medium heat until dark brown in colour, stopping before it starts to smoke. Remove from the heat and pour in the salt and half the cream. The mixture will bubble violently, so be careful and go slowly.

Once the mixture has settled, add the remaining cream followed by the butter. If the mixture is lumpy, put the pan back on the heat and stir until smooth. Pour into a heatproof jug to cool and stir in the crème fraîche. Mix in the chopped pecans, reserving a few for decoration, then spread evenly over the cooled tart shell.

To make the chocolate layer, put the cream and sugar into a medium pan and bring to a simmer. Put the chocolate into a medium bowl. Pour the cream mixture over the chocolate and leave for a few minutes before stirring in concentric circles, starting into the centre and working your way out. Once you have a smooth ganache, stir in the softened butter.

Pour over the chilled tart and top with the reserved pecans. Allow the chocolate to set before serving.

GINGER AND CHAI PANNACOTTA TARTS

This was one of the first ideas I had when writing this book. Chai tea is something that I love, it's warm and comforting and full of spice, and I really wanted to translate that into a tart. The flavour of the tea comes through beautifully in the pannacotta filling and is balanced with the chocolate that coats the tart — a perfect dish to serve for an afternoon tea.

MAKES 6

BUTTER, FOR GREASING

FLOUR, FOR DUSTING

½ QUANTITY SWEET PASTRY
   (PAGE 170) OR 500G SHOP-BOUGHT
   SWEET SHORTCRUST PASTRY

50G DARK CHOCOLATE (AT LEAST
   60–70% COCOA SOLIDS), BROKEN
   INTO PIECES

30G STEM GINGER, CHOPPED

COCOA POWDER, FOR DUSTING

FOR THE PANNACOTTA FILLING

200ML DOUBLE CREAM

130ML MILK

35G SUGAR

2 CHAI TEA BAGS

2 GELATINE LEAVES

ICE-COLD WATER, FOR SOAKING

Lightly grease six individual tartlet tins. Lightly flour the work surface and the rolling pin, and roll out the pastry until 3–4mm thick. Cut out six rounds of pastry about 4cm wider in diameter than the tartlet tins. Line the tins with the pastry, trimming off any excess, and chill for 15 minutes or until firm. Preheat the oven to 180°C (160°C fan oven) gas mark 4.

Line the pastry shells with baking parchment and fill with a layer of baking beans or rice. Bake for 15 minutes. Remove the beans and parchment and bake for a further 10 minutes or until golden. Leave the pastry shells to cool.

Meanwhile, melt the chocolate in a microwave or a heatproof bowl over a pan of gently simmering water, making sure the base of the bowl doesn't touch the water. Once the shells are cool, brush the insides with the melted chocolate and sprinkle the glacé ginger over the bases. Put the tarts in the fridge to set.

To make the filling, put the cream, milk, sugar and chai tea bags into a small pan and bring just to the boil. Remove from the heat, cover and allow to infuse for 30 minutes.

Put the gelatine into a small bowl of ice-cold water for 10 minutes. Once the gelatine has softened, remove the tea bags from the cream, then bring the cream mixture back to a very gentle simmer. Add the gelatine and stir to melt. Remove from the heat and allow to cool, stirring now and then to prevent it setting. Once the mixture has cooled to room temperature, divide it equally among the tart shells. Chill until set, about 4 hours. To serve, remove from the fridge and dust with cocoa powder.

TIP

To make these even more elegant place a thin strip of card or paper over the tart before dusting with cocoa. When removed it will leave a lovely pattern.

CHOCOLATE AND ORANGE PORTUGUESE CUSTARD TARTS

Portuguese custard tarts are so simple — just puff pastry and custard — but they are more delicious than those few ingredients might suggest. Using store-bought pastry makes them a breeze to put together. The pastry is crisp and the custard deliciously creamy but, unlike the traditional version, I flavour the custard with orange and finish the tarts with a grating of chocolate.

MAKES 12

BUTTER, FOR GREASING
100ML DOUBLE CREAM
175ML MILK
ZEST OF 1 ORANGE
2 TABLESPOONS PLAIN FLOUR, PLUS
   EXTRA FOR DUSTING
3 EGG YOLKS
100G CASTER SUGAR
½ QUANTITY ROUGH PUFF PASTRY
   (PAGE 172) OR 375G SHOP-BOUGHT
   PUFF PASTRY, THAWED IF FROZEN
20G DARK CHOCOLATE (AT LEAST
   60–70% COCOA SOLIDS)

Preheat the oven to 200°C (180°C fan oven) gas mark 6 and lightly grease a 12-cup muffin pan. Put the double cream, milk and orange zest into a medium pan set over medium heat and bring just to the boil.

Meanwhile, whisk the flour, egg yolks and sugar together until pale and smooth. Pour the hot cream over the egg mixture, whisking constantly. Pour the custard back into the pan and cook over low heat, stirring constantly, until it thickens enough to coat the back of a wooden spoon. Pour into a heatproof jug and press a piece of clingfilm onto the surface. Chill until needed.

Lightly flour the work surface and the rolling pin, and roll out the puff pastry into a 2–3mm thick rectangle. Roll up the pastry from the short end into a tight coil and cut into twelve 1cm slices. Place the slices onto the floured surface and roll each out thinly. Using a 10cm cookie cutter, cut out rounds of pastry. Press the pastry rounds into the prepared muffin cups, then fill each tart with custard.

Bake in the preheated oven for 20 minutes or until the pastry is golden and the custard is set. Remove from the oven and allow to cool in the pan before grating the chocolate over the tarts and serving.

STRAWBERRY TARTS

This is my version of the classic Bakewell Tart, a frangipane filling baked on top of a layer of jam in a shortcrust pastry base. I have retained the basic idea, but I have added fresh strawberries to the top of the tart for flavour, texture and appearance.

MAKES 8

170G UNSALTED BUTTER, AT ROOM
   TEMPERATURE, PLUS EXTRA FOR
   GREASING

½ QUANTITY SWEET PASTRY
   (PAGE 170) OR 500G SHOP-BOUGHT
   SWEET SHORTCRUST PASTRY

FLOUR, FOR DUSTING

170G CASTER SUGAR

4 EGGS

280G GROUND ALMONDS

200G STRAWBERRY JAM

150G STRAWBERRIES, DICED

ICING SUGAR, FOR DUSTING, OR
   MELTED APRICOT JAM, FOR
   BRUSHING

Lightly grease eight 10cm individual tartlet tins, set aside. Take the chilled pastry from the fridge and allow it to rest for 10 minutes. Lightly flour the work surface and the rolling pin, and roll out the pastry until 3–4mm thick. Cut out rounds about 14cm in diameter and gently press into the prepared tart tins. Trim off the excess pastry and chill for 15 minutes. Preheat the oven to 200°C (180°C fan oven) gas mark 6.

To make the frangipane filling, beat the butter and sugar together until light and fluffy, about 5 minutes. Beat in the eggs one at a time until fully combined, then stir in the almonds.

Line the tarts with a piece of baking parchment and fill with a layer of baking beans or rice, then put on a baking tray. Bake for 15 minutes. Remove the baking parchment and beans, then bake for a further 10 minutes or until the tarts are beginning to turn golden. Reduce the oven to 180°C (160°C fan oven) gas mark 4.

Remove the tarts from the oven and divide the jam evenly among the tarts. Add the frangipane, spreading evenly across the pastry cases. Top with a sprinkling of diced strawberry. Bake for 20–25 minutes or until the frangipane filling has turned a light golden brown. Allow to cool, then dust with a little icing sugar or brush with a little melted apricot jam.

CURD TARTS

Many people haven't heard of this traditional Yorkshire tart, though I have strong memories of eating it as a child. The main ingredient is curds, a product created during the cheese-making process. The flavour of curds is mild, so currants and spices are added to make a delicious end result — think of it as a Yorkshire twist on cheesecake.

SERVES 6

2 PINTS WHOLE MILK

2 TABLESPOONS VEGETARIAN RENNET

100G UNSALTED BUTTER, AT ROOM
  TEMPERATURE, PLUS EXTRA FOR
  GREASING

FLOUR, FOR DUSTING

½ QUANTITY SWEET PASTRY
  (PAGE 170) OR 500G SHOP-BOUGHT
  SWEET SHORTCRUST PASTRY

50G CASTER SUGAR

1 LARGE EGG

1 TABLESPOON DOUBLE CREAM

25G GROUND ALMONDS

ZEST OF 1 LEMON

½ TEASPOON GROUND MIXED SPICE

¼ TEASPOON FRESHLY GRATED NUTMEG

PINCH OF SALT

100G CURRANTS

The night before you want to bake the tarts, put the milk into a medium pan set over medium heat and bring to 37°C (luke warm). Remove from the heat and stir in the rennet, then allow to set for 1 hour.

Line a fine sieve with muslin and set over a bowl. Break up the curds a little with a fork and pour the mixture into the sieve. Allow to drain overnight, leaving you with the curds in the sieve.

Lightly grease six individual tartlet tins. Lightly flour the work surface and the rolling pin, then roll out the chilled shortcrust pastry until 3–4mm thick. Cut out six rounds, about 5cm wider in diameter than the tins, and use to line the prepared tins, cutting off any excess.

Chill the pastry shells for 15 minutes or until firm. Preheat the oven to 200°C (180°C fan oven) gas mark 6. Line the tarts with baking parchment and fill with a layer of baking beans or rice. Bake for 10 minutes. Remove the parchment and beans, then bake for a further 5 minutes or until lightly golden.

Using an electric mixer, beat the butter and sugar together until light and fluffy, about 5 minutes. Add the egg and cream, and beat to combine; don't worry if the mixture looks curdled, that's to be expected.

Add the almonds, lemon zest, spices and salt, and beat to combine. Finally, add the currants and curds, and lightly mix together until the curds are just evenly distributed. Divide the curd mixture between the tarts and bake for 15–20 minutes or until the filling turns golden around the edges. Allow to cool before serving.

APPLE AND PECAN TART

Frangipane is a basic mix of sugar, butter, eggs and ground nuts – normally almonds – but in this tart I have used a nut with so much more flavour: pecans. The wonderful thing about this recipe is that it is so adaptable; you can take the basic recipe and play around with so many variations. Just change the nuts and filling to suit your taste. You could try ground almonds instead of pecans, and pear with cherry jam as the filling.

SERVES 8

85G UNSALTED BUTTER, AT ROOM TEMPERATURE, PLUS EXTRA FOR GREASING

½ QUANTITY SWEET PASTRY (PAGE 170) OR 500G SHOP-BOUGHT SWEET SHORTCRUST PASTRY

FLOUR, FOR DUSTING

140G PECANS, PLUS A FEW EXTRA FOR DECORATION

85G CASTER SUGAR

2 EGGS, LIGHTLY BEATEN

5 TABLESPOONS GOLDEN SYRUP

1 LARGE GRANNY SMITH APPLE, PEELED, CORED AND DICED

Lightly grease a 35 x 12cm fluted rectangular tart tin, preferably with a removable base. Take the chilled pastry from the fridge and allow it to rest for 10 minutes. Lightly flour the work surface and the rolling pin, and roll the pastry until 3–4mm thick. Gently lift the pastry over the tart tin and press into the sides and the corners of the tin. Trim the edges and chill the tart for 15 minutes to firm it up. Preheat the oven to 200°C (180°C fan oven) gas mark 6.

Put the pecans into the bowl of a food processor and pulse until very finely chopped, stopping before they turn to a paste. Remove the pecans and add the butter and sugar to the processor. Pulse until the mixture is light and fluffy, 2 minutes, then add the eggs, one at a time, and pulse until combined. Mix in the pecans. Set aside.

Line the tart with baking parchment and fill with a layer of baking beans or rice. Bake for 15 minutes. Remove the beans and parchment, and bake for a further 10 minutes or until the tart is beginning to turn golden. Reduce the oven temperature to 180°C (160°C fan oven) gas mark 4.

Remove the tart from the oven and spread the golden syrup and diced apple evenly across the base, reserving a few pieces of apple. Add the pecan mixture and spread evenly across the tart.

Sprinkle the reserved apple and pecans across the tart and bake for 20–25 minutes or until the tart has started to brown around the edges of the frangipane. Allow to cool before serving.

SEASONAL FRUIT GALETTE

Galettes are freeform tarts: no tins or pans needed, just pastry and fruit — rustic but very tasty indeed. You can use almost any fruit, but it's always best to use what's in season. That way you get the best tasting result possible. Although wonderful served plain, it is also excellent with cream or a scoop of ice cream.

SERVES 6

FLOUR, FOR DUSTING
½ QUANTITY SHORTCRUST PASTRY
   (PAGE 171) OR 500G SHOP-BOUGHT
   SHORTCRUST PASTRY
ABOUT 300G FRESH FRUIT SUCH AS
   APPLES, NECTARINES, APRICOTS ETC
1 TABLESPOON PLAIN FLOUR
JUICE OF ½ LEMON
3 TABLESPOONS CASTER SUGAR
10G BUTTER, IN SMALL PIECES
1 EGG, LIGHTLY BEATEN

Preheat the oven to 200°C (180°C fan oven) gas mark 6 and line a baking tray with baking parchment. Lightly flour the work surface and the rolling pin, and roll out the chilled pastry into a circle about 35–40cm in diameter. Put onto the prepared baking tray.

Peel and core the fruit, then cut into thin slices, toss with the flour and lemon juice, coating evenly. Put the fruit into the centre of the pastry and sprinkle with 2 tablespoons of the sugar. Dot the butter across the fruit and fold the edge around the fruit, pleating to make it fit.

Brush the pastry with the beaten egg and sprinkle with the remaining sugar. Bake in the preheated oven for 45–50 minutes or until the pastry is golden and the filling is bubbling. Allow to cool slightly before serving.

PEAR TARTE TATIN

Tarte Tatin is a French classic, and rightly so: caramelised apples in a puff pastry case are a delicious combination. So too is my version using pears in a lightly spiced caramel. The original recipe was created at Hotel Tatin in France in 1898 by one of the Tatin sisters. The story goes that she baked an apple pie upside down by mistake one day, but found that the resulting dish was hugely popular with the hotel guests. It soon became their signature dish. Once the tart is finished it will be very hot – too hot to eat, so allow it to sit for a few minutes until it is just nicely warm. To serve, I would suggest a scoop of Vanilla Ice Cream (page 154).

SERVES 6

3–4 LARGE COMICE PEARS

50G UNSALTED BUTTER

50G CASTER SUGAR

2 WHOLE STAR ANISE

4 CARDAMOM PODS

FLOUR, FOR DUSTING

½ QUANTITY ROUGH PUFF PASTRY
(PAGE 172) OR 225G SHOP-BOUGHT
PUFF PASTRY, THAWED IF FROZEN

Preheat the oven to 220°C (200°C fan oven) gas mark 7. Core, peel and cut the pears in half. Put the butter in a 20cm ovenproof frying pan and add the caster sugar, star anise and cardamom. Cook over high heat until the caramel turns a dark brown and smells gently spiced. Turn the heat down to medium.

Add the prepared pears, cut side up, and cook for 10 minutes or until caramelised. Remove the pan from the heat and allow it to cool slightly.

Lightly flour the work surface and the rolling pin, and roll out the chilled puff pastry to about 4mm thick. Cut out a round of pastry about 25cm in diameter. Put the pastry on top of the pears and tuck the excess under the pears around the edge. Bake for 25 minutes or until the pastry is puffed and golden.

Allow the tart to rest in the pan for 15–20 minutes to cool slightly before turning out onto a plate to serve.

BLACKBERRY MILLEFEUILLE

Millefeuille, or 'thousand leaves' is a French classic: crisp and delicate puff pastry filled with layers of pastry cream. When it is well made, it is a thing of beauty. This is my version, using fresh fruit and whipped cream to make for an easier and lighter take on the classic.

SERVES 4

ABOUT 35G CASTER SUGAR
FLOUR, FOR DUSTING
1 QUANTITY ROUGH PUFF PASTRY
   (PAGE 172) OR 375G SHOP-BOUGHT
   PUFF PASTRY, THAWED IF FROZEN
ICING SUGAR, TO DECORATE

FOR THE FILLING
100ML DOUBLE CREAM
1 TEASPOON VANILLA BEAN PASTE
300G BLACKBERRIES

Preheat the oven to 200°C (180°C fan oven) gas mark 6 and line a baking tray with baking parchment. Sprinkle the work surface with about 1 tablespoon caster sugar to give it a thin dusting.

Lightly flour the rolling pin, and roll out the chilled pastry into a rectangle 2–3mm thick. Transfer to the baking tray. Sprinkle the top of the pastry with a thin layer of caster sugar and cover with a piece of baking parchment.

Place a similar close-fitting baking tray on top of the baking parchment. This is to stop the pastry from puffing up in the oven, as you want thin, delicate sheets of pastry. Bake for 20 minutes. Remove the two baking trays together from the oven. Turn the whole contraption upside down and remove what was the bottom baking tray and the visible layer of baking parchment. Sprinkle a little more caster sugar onto the pastry, then put it back into the oven and bake for 15–20 minutes or until caramelised. Remove from the oven and allow to cool.

To make the filling, whisk the double cream and vanilla bean paste until it forms medium-firm peaks.

To assemble, use a long, serrated knife to cut out twelve rectangles of pastry about 6 × 12cm each. Put four pieces of pastry onto serving plates and arrange the blackberries around the outside. Fill the centre with vanilla cream. Repeat with a second piece of pastry and top each millefeuille with a final piece of pastry. Dust with a little icing sugar and serve.

PUMPKIN PIE

This pie is quintessentially American, normally eaten in the autumn and winter and classically served at Thanksgiving. Although we don't celebrate Thanksgiving in the UK, if it meant more pumpkin pie I would be happy to import the holiday here. As with most custard-based pies and tarts, remove it from the oven when set around the outside but still a little wobbly in the centre, as the filling will continue to cook as it cools. Serve with maple syrup-flavoured cream, a classic American combination.

SERVES 8–10

425G PUMPKIN PURÉE (AVAILABLE IN SOME SUPERMARKETS, HEALTH FOOD SHOPS AND ONLINE)

FLOUR, FOR DUSTING

½ QUANTITY SHORTCRUST PASTRY (PAGE 171) OR 500G SHOP-BOUGHT SHORTCRUST PASTRY

1 LARGE EGG

2 LARGE EGG YOLKS

170G CASTER SUGAR

¼ TEASPOON SALT

1½ TEASPOONS GROUND CINNAMON

1 TEASPOON GROUND GINGER

¼ TEASPOON GROUND CLOVES

250ML SOURED CREAM

WHIPPED CREAM FLAVOURED WITH MAPLE SYRUP, TO SERVE

Lightly flour the work surface and the rolling pin, and roll out the chilled pastry until 3–4mm thick. Use to line a 23cm pie dish, then trim the excess, leaving a 2.5cm overhang. Using your fingers, take the overhang and roll it under itself, allowing the rolled edge to rest on the edge of the pie dish. Crimp the edge between your fingers and thumb, then chill for 30 minutes or until firm. Preheat the oven to 200°C (180°C fan oven) gas mark 6.

Line the prepared pastry shell with baking parchment and fill with baking beans or rice. Bake for 20 minutes. Remove the parchment and beans, then bake for a further 10 minutes, until the pastry is starting to colour.

Meanwhile, make the filling by mixing all the remaining ingredients and the puréed pumpkin together until smooth.

Remove the part-baked pastry shell from the oven and fill with the pumpkin filling. Reduce the oven temperature to 180°C (160°C fan oven) gas mark 4 and bake for a further 30–40 minutes or until set. Serve cold with whipped cream flavoured with a little maple syrup.

BOURBON PECAN PIE

Pecan pie is one of those classic American recipes that hasn't really made the jump across the Atlantic as it should have. It's pure autumn in a recipe: warm, caramel, pecans, pie crust and bourbon, everything about it makes me want to curl up in front of a fire and stay out of the cold. Because it is on the sweet side, I have added orange zest to make it a little fresher, but you could omit this if you prefer something a little more classic in flavour.

SERVES 8–10

½ QUANTITY SHORTCRUST PASTRY
   (PAGE 171) OR 500G SHOP-BOUGHT
   SHORTCRUST PASTRY, CHILLED
FLOUR, FOR DUSTING
200G PECAN HALVES
70G BUTTER, MELTED AND COOLED
200G DARK BROWN SUGAR
ZEST OF ½ ORANGE (OPTIONAL)
360G GOLDEN SYRUP
4 EGGS
1 TEASPOON VANILLA EXTRACT
2 TABLESPOONS BOURBON (OPTIONAL)
¼ TEASPOON SALT

Remove the chilled pastry from the fridge and allow it to rest for 10 minutes. Lightly flour the work surface and the rolling pin, and roll the pastry until 3–4mm thick.

Line a 23cm pie dish with the pastry and trim the excess, leaving a 2.5cm overhang. Using your fingers, take the overhang and roll it under itself allowing the rolled edge to rest on the edge of the pie dish. Crimp the edge between the finger and thumb of one hand and the index finger of the other, then chill for 30 minutes or until firm. Preheat the oven to 180°C (160°C fan oven) gas mark 4.

Line the prepared pastry shell with baking parchment and a layer of baking beans or rice. Bake for 15 minutes. Remove the foil and beans, then bake for a further 10 minutes or until the pie begins to turn golden.

Meanwhile, make the filling. Reserve one third of the pecans to decorate the top, then roughly chop the remainder. In a medium bowl whisk together all the remaining ingredients until combined.

Scatter the tart base with the chopped pecan nuts, then pour over the filling and top with the reserved pecan halves. Put the pie back in the oven and bake for 50 minutes–1 hour or until the filling is set. Allow to cool before serving.

STREUSEL APPLE PIE

This is like eating a cross between apple pie and apple crumble — no bad thing let me tell you! Of course a classic apple pie is also wonderful, but the little twist this includes is one of my absolute favourite ways of serving the iconic traditional dessert. Instead of a pastry top it uses a streusel crumble topping. It takes only a little more effort, and I think it's totally worth it.

SERVES 8

FLOUR, FOR DUSTING
½ QUANTITY SHORTCRUST PASTRY
   (PAGE 171) OR 500G SHOP-BOUGHT
   SHORTCRUST PASTRY, CHILLED

FOR THE STREUSEL TOPPING
140G PLAIN FLOUR
100G CASTER SUGAR
110G BUTTER

FOR THE FILLING
1.3KG EATING APPLES (I PREFER
   GRANNY SMITHS)
1 TEASPOON LEMON JUICE
15G CASTER SUGAR
1½ TEASPOONS GROUND CINNAMON
½ TEASPOON FRESHLY GRATED NUTMEG
½ TEASPOON GROUND GINGER
3 TABLESPOONS PLAIN FLOUR
PINCH OF SALT
15G BUTTER, IN SMALL PIECES

To make the streusel topping, sift the flour and sugar together then rub in the butter using your fingertips or a pastry blender. Gather the dough together, then chill until needed.

Lightly flour the work surface and the rolling pin, and roll out the chilled shortcrust pastry to fit a 23cm pie dish. Line with the dough and trim the excess leaving a 2.5cm overhang. Roll the excess pastry under itself to form the pie's edge. To crimp the pie, pinch the thumb and forefinger of one hand together and, using the index finger of your other hand, press the pie edge between your fingers to form a simple scallop. Chill for 30 minutes. Preheat the oven to 200°C (180°C fan oven) gas mark 6.

Line the prepared pastry shell with baking parchment and fill with a layer of baking beans or rice. Bake for 20 minutes. Remove the parchment and beans, then bake for a further 10 minutes or until the pie begins to turn golden.

To make the filling, peel, core and slice the apples, then put in a large bowl with the lemon juice, sugar, cinnamon, nutmeg, ginger, flour and salt. Mix well.

Add the filling to the pastry shell and dot with the butter. Bake for 15 minutes, then open the oven and reduce the temperature to 180°C (160°C fan oven) gas mark 4. Break the streusel topping into little pieces and spread it across the top of the pie. Bake for another 45–50 minutes or until the filling is bubbling and the pastry is golden. If the pastry is browning too fast, cover the pie loosely with a piece of foil. Allow to cool for 20–30 minutes before serving.

INDIVIDUAL BAKED ALASKA

The traditional Baked Alaska was always a firm family favourite, and it was my older brother's dessert of choice every birthday — instead of cake! Madness, I know! Instead of sticking to tradition I have taken the idea and turned it into individual tartlets. One of the great things about this recipe is how it can be adapted; by changing the ice cream and filling you have endless variations at your fingertips. Why not try fresh raspberries with chocolate ice cream?

MAKES 8

BUTTER, FOR GREASING
½ QUANTITY SWEET PASTRY
  (PAGE 170) OR 500G SHOP-BOUGHT
  SWEET SHORTCRUST PASTRY
FLOUR, FOR DUSTING
320G GRANULATED SUGAR
350G VANILLA ICE CREAM (PAGE 154)
120G JAM OR LEMON CURD
120G EGG WHITES

Lightly grease eight individual tartlet tins. Remove the pastry from the fridge and allow it to rest for 10 minutes. Lightly flour the work surface and the rolling pin, and roll out the pastry until 3–4mm thick. Cut out eight rounds, about 4cm wider in diameter than the tins. Use the rounds to line the prepared tart tins, trimming off any excess.

Chill the pastry for 15 minutes or until firm. Preheat the oven to 180°C (160°C fan oven) gas mark 4. Line the tarts with baking parchment and fill with a layer of baking beans or rice. Bake for 15 minutes. Remove the parchment and beans and bake for a further 10 minutes or until golden brown. Remove and set aside to cool.

To make the meringue, put 100ml water and the sugar into a small pan and set over medium heat. Bring to the boil and have a sugar thermometer ready. As the syrup reaches about 115°C put the egg whites into a clean grease-free bowl (this is best done using a freestanding electric mixer) and whisk on high speed.

Once the syrup has reached 121°C, remove it from the heat and, with the mixer still running, pour the syrup in a slow stream down the side of the bowl, avoiding the whisk.

To assemble the tartlets, put a scoop of ice cream in the centre of each tart shell and surround with jam or lemon curd. Put the meringue into a piping bag fitted with a large plain piping nozzle and pipe in spiral circles starting on the outside and working inwards, covering all the ice cream.

You can either serve immediately or, if you prefer a more traditional finish, use a blowtorch to lightly toast the meringue. If you don't have a blowtorch, you can put the tarts under the grill for a minute or two until the meringue is lightly golden.

APPLE AND BLUEBERRY KING'S CAKE

Galette de Rois, or King's Cake, is traditionally served in France on the day of epiphany, 6 January, but there's no reason not to eat it all year round. Normally, it is just filled with an almond mixture, but I have given it a little modern twist and added a layer of apple purée and blueberries, to help cut the richness of the frangipane and to add another layer of flavour. Depending on the time of year, you could fill with any manner of ingredients, from raspberries to chopped chocolate.

SERVES 8

FLOUR, FOR DUSTING
2 QUANTITIES ROUGH PUFF PASTRY
  (PAGE 172) OR 500G SHOP-BOUGHT
  PUFF PASTRY, THAWED IF FROZEN
1 EGG YOLK MIXED WITH
  1 TABLESPOON WATER

FOR THE FRANGIPANE

50G UNSALTED BUTTER, SOFTENED
50G CASTER SUGAR
1 LARGE EGG
50G GROUND ALMONDS

FOR THE FRUIT FILLING

1 LARGE BRAEBURN APPLE
1 TABLESPOON ICING SUGAR,
  OR TO TASTE
100G BLUEBERRIES

Preheat the oven to 180°C (160°C fan oven) gas mark 4 and line two baking trays with baking parchment. To make the filling wrap the apple in foil and bake until tender, about 45 minutes. Remove the core and purée the flesh with a hand blender, then pass it through a sieve. Add icing sugar to taste.

To make the frangipane, beat the butter and sugar together until light and fluffy. Beat in the egg a little at a time, followed by the almonds. Chill the apple purée and frangipane while you make the pastry layers.

Lightly flour the work surface and the rolling pin, and roll out the pastry until 3mm thick, then cut out two discs 30cm in diameter. Put onto the baking trays and chill for 30 minutes.

When ready to assemble, spread the frangipane in an even layer over one of the pastry rounds, leaving a 2.5cm border. Spread the apple purée onto the frangipane and top with the blueberries. Lay the second disc of pastry on top and seal the edges. Score the top with a knife in a pattern, making sure not to cut through the pastry. Either leave the edge as a simple round or use a knife to create a scalloped edge. Chill for a further 30 minutes. Preheat the oven to 220°C (200°C fan oven) gas mark 7.

Brush the chilled cake with the egg yolk and water, and bake for 25–30 minutes or until golden.

PUMPKIN PIE ECLAIRS

Normally eclairs come in the classic flavours of chocolate, coffee and sometimes pistachio, but I wanted to try something a little more unusual, so I decided to take the classic American Pumpkin Pie and use those flavours to fill eclairs. If you prefer something more traditional, use the choux pastry recipe and fill with either simply whipped cream or Pastry Cream (page 165).

MAKES 12

60G UNSALTED BUTTER, CUT INTO
   SMALL PIECES
¼ TEASPOON CASTER SUGAR
¼ TEASPOON SALT
85G PLAIN FLOUR
2–3 EGGS, PLUS EXTRA FOR GLAZING

FOR THE FILLING
400G PUMPKIN PURÉE (AVAILABLE IN
   SOME SUPERMARKETS, HEALTH FOOD
   STORES AND ONLINE)
250ML WHOLE MILK
1 TEASPOON GROUND CINNAMON
½ TEASPOON GROUND GINGER
8 EGG YOLKS
2 TABLESPOONS PLAIN FLOUR
90G CASTER SUGAR
2 TEASPOONS VANILLA EXTRACT

FOR THE GLAZE
1 250G ICING SUGAR
1–2 DROPS EGG-YELLOW FOOD
   COLOURING

To make the filling, put the milk, pumpkin purée and spices in a medium pan over medium-high heat until it just comes to the boil. Meanwhile, whisk the egg yolks, flour, sugar and vanilla extract until combined and lightened.

Pour the pumpkin mixture over the egg mixture, whisking constantly. Pour back into the pan and cook until the mixture has thickened, whisking constantly. Pour the mixture into a medium bowl and cover with clingfilm. Chill until needed.

Preheat the oven to 220°C (200°C fan oven) gas mark 7 and line two baking trays with baking parchment. Put the butter, sugar, salt and 140ml water into a medium pan set over medium heat and bring to the boil. Take off the heat and tip in the flour, beating with a wooden spoon until combined. Put back on the heat and beat the dough for about 30 seconds or until it comes away from the sides of the pan.

Tip the dough into a medium bowl and beat vigorously until no longer hot or steaming. Beat in the eggs one at a time until the dough is smooth and shiny and falls from a wooden spoon forming a V-shaped ribbon. Put the dough into a piping bag fitted with a large round piping nozzle and pipe into 15cm lines on the baking trays. Brush the top of each eclair with a little beaten egg.

Bake for 25–30 minutes or until golden brown. Remove from the oven and make two or three small holes in each éclair, using a small star-shaped piping nozzle to release the steam. Fit a piping bag with the star-shaped piping nozzle and fill with the pumpkin pastry cream. Use to fill each eclair.

To make the glaze, mix the icing sugar with 7 tablespoons water and the food colouring until smooth. Dip the top of each eclair into the glaze and allow to dry before serving.

DESSERTS

PEACH AND BLUEBERRY COBBLER

Apart from eating fruit plain, I think a crumble or cobbler is the perfect way to showcase fruit that is in season and at its best. It is also very easy to put together, so if you should come across a batch of beautiful fruit at the farmers' market, there is no reason not to just whip up a delicious dessert for dinner that evening.

SERVES 4–6

850G RIPE PEACHES

80G BLUEBERRIES

2 TEASPOONS LEMON JUICE

100G CASTER SUGAR

30G PLAIN FLOUR

SINGLE CREAM OR VANILLA ICE CREAM
   (PAGE 154), TO SERVE

FOR THE COBBLER

150G SELF-RAISING FLOUR

55G BUTTER

100G CASTER SUGAR

120ML BUTTERMILK

Preheat the oven to 180°C (160°C fan oven) gas mark 4. Put the peaches into a bowl of boiling water for up to 1 minute (very ripe peaches will take less time). Remove and cool under cold water. Use the tip of a knife to loosen the skin, then peel it off. Cut the peaches in half to remove the stone then cut into slices.

In a bowl, mix together the peaches, blueberries, lemon juice, sugar and flour. Tip into a 1 litre ovenproof dish and bake for 20 minutes while you make the cobbler topping.

In the bowl of a food processor, pulse the flour, butter and sugar together until the mixture resembles very fine breadcrumbs. Pulse in the buttermilk just until you have a soft dough. (Alternatively, put the flour into a medium bowl and rub in the butter until it resembles fine breadcrumbs, then stir in the sugar. Pour in the buttermilk and mix gently together until you have a soft dough.)

Remove the dish of fruit from the oven and add the topping in large spoonfuls. Bake for a further 40–50 minutes or until the cobbler topping has browned and the fruit is bubbling. Serve drizzled with cream or a large scoop of vanilla ice cream.

ALMONDINE

This recipe was inspired during the time I spent in the kitchens at Raymond Blanc's restaurant, Le Manoir – a wonderful experience that I will always remember. They served a version of this dish with poached pear and ginger crème anglaise. This recipe is basically a frangipane baked into a mould and topped with crumble and whatever filling you like, such as jams, compote, or even mincemeat, for a Christmas-themed version. Served plain they can be eaten like little cakes, but serve them slightly warm with Crème Anglaise and fresh fruit, and you have a delicious dessert.

MAKES 12

40G UNSALTED BUTTER, COLD,
   PLUS EXTRA FOR GREASING
40G DEMERARA SUGAR
60G PLAIN FLOUR
FILLING OF YOUR CHOICE, SUCH
   AS JAM, CHOCOLATE, MINCEMEAT
CRÈME ANGLAISE (PAGE 164),
   TO SERVE (OPTIONAL)

FOR THE FRANGIPANE

200G UNSALTED BUTTER, SOFTENED
200G CASTER SUGAR
200G GROUND ALMONDS
2 EGGS
A FEW DROPS OF ALMOND EXTRACT
100G CORNFLOUR

Preheat the oven to 180°C (160°C fan oven) gas mark 4 and lightly grease a 12-cup muffin pan. Rub the butter into the sugar and flour using your fingertips or a pastry blender until it resembles fine breadcrumbs. Chill.

To make the frangipane, beat the butter until smooth and creamy, then add the sugar and almonds, and beat until just combined. Beat in the eggs and almond extract, then fold in the cornflour.

Divide the frangipane mixture among the prepared muffin cups, smoothing the mixture with a spoon. Sprinkle the crumble topping around the edge of each and put a small spoonful of your choice of filling in the centre. Bake for 20–25 minutes or until a cocktail stick inserted into the centre (avoiding the filling) comes out clean. Serve warm with Crème Anglaise or cold.

BANANA CREAM PIE

Rather than allow the classic Banana Cream Pie to rest on its laurels, I have had a play around and made it my way. I did away with the pastry in favour of a biscuit-crumb base, and instead of custard I'm using ice cream. In the recipe I simply use Vanilla Ice Cream, but if you want to you can make it even more exciting by using my Popcorn Ice Cream (page 152).

SERVES 8

90G BUTTER, PLUS EXTRA FOR
    GREASING
250G SWEET OAT BISCUITS
300ML VANILLA ICE CREAM
    (PAGE 154), SOFTENED
75G GRANULATED SUGAR
PINCH OF SALT
510ML DOUBLE CREAM
½ TEASPOON VANILLA BEAN PASTE
3 LARGE BANANAS, SLICED
50G HAZELNUTS, ROUGHLY
    CHOPPED

Preheat the oven to 180°C (160°C fan oven) gas mark 4 and lightly grease a 23cm tart tin, preferably one with a removable base. Put the biscuits into a food processor and pulse until they resemble breadcrumbs. (Alternatively, put them in a plastic bag and crush with a rolling pin.) Tip into a bowl.

Melt 85g of the butter in a microwave or small saucepan. Pour over the biscuit crumbs and mix together evenly. Press into the base and sides the tart tin. Bake for 15 minutes or until the edges are golden. Cool in the tin on a wire rack.

Spread the vanilla ice cream evenly across the cooled base of the pie and put in the freezer until the ice cream is firm.

In a medium pan, melt the sugar over medium heat until dark brown in colour, stopping before it starts to smoke. Remove from the heat and add the salt, remaining 5g butter and 60ml double cream – the mixture will bubble violently so be careful and go slowly. Once the mixture has settled and is smooth, pour into a small bowl or heatproof jug to cool.

When ready to serve, whip the remaining cream with the vanilla bean paste until medium-strong peaks form. To assemble, scatter the banana slices and chopped hazelnuts across the ice cream (reserving a little of each for decoration). Drizzle with the caramel, then top with the whipped cream and the reserved banana and nuts. Serve immediately.

INDIVIDUAL APPLE CRUMBLES

Apple crumble always seems to be one of those desserts that your mum makes better than anyone else. I love nothing more than going home to visit my parents and being served a home-cooked meal finished off with the dessert I had most as a child – it's pure nostalgia. My individual crumbles are slightly different because they have an oaty topping – I think they're just as delicious as the version I grew up with!

SERVES 4

200G PLAIN FLOUR

150G CASTER SUGAR

90G PORRIDGE OATS

PINCH OF SALT

175G UNSALTED BUTTER, CHILLED AND CUT INTO CUBES

1KG BRAMLEY APPLES

50G CASTER SUGAR

1 TEASPOON GROUND CINNAMON

Put the flour in a medium bowl with the sugar, oats and salt and mix to combine. Add the butter and rub into the flour mixture with your fingertips or a pastry blender until evenly distributed. Gather the crumble mixture into one solid mass and wrap in clingfilm. Chill for 1 hour.

Preheat the oven to 200°C (180°C fan oven) gas mark 6. Peel, core and chop the apples into chunks. Toss together with the sugar and cinnamon, coating evenly, and divide equally among four individual ovenproof dishes.

Remove the crumble from the fridge and break it up into irregular chunks with your fingers. Divide it among the four dishes. Bake the crumbles for 20–25 minutes or until the topping is golden and the filling is bubbling.

MANGO AND PASSION FRUIT PAVLOVA

Pavlova makes a very impressive dessert; it is colourful and has a great texture: crisp on the outside and pillowy soft in the centre. It is sweet, so the fresh fruit helps to balance out the sugar. Instead of using a simple whipped cream as the topping I have opted to use a slightly richer mascarpone-based cream, which makes the light dessert feel a little more special.

SERVES 10–12

225G EGG WHITES, FROM ABOUT
    6 EGGS
325G CASTER SUGAR
1 TABLESPOON CORNFLOUR
2 TEASPOONS WHITE VINEGAR

FOR THE TOPPING
200G DOUBLE CREAM
1 TABLESPOON ICING SUGAR
250G MASCARPONE, AT ROOM
    TEMPERATURE
2 MANGOES, PEELED AND DICED
3 PASSION FRUITS

Preheat the oven to 110°C (90°C fan oven) gas mark ¼ and line a baking tray with baking parchment. Draw a 30cm circle onto the paper, then invert the paper so that the marks are on the underside. Put the egg whites into a clean, grease-free bowl (this is best done using a freestanding electric mixer) and whisk until they form firm peaks. Add the sugar in a slow stream, continuing to whisk until the meringue is stiff and shiny.

In a small bowl, mix the cornflour and vinegar together. Add this to the meringue mixture and whisk until just fully combined.

Spoon the meringue into the circle and bake for 1½ hours or until crisp on the outside and very lightly coloured. Turn off the oven and allow the pavlova to cool completely.

To make the topping, whisk the cream to soft peaks, add the icing sugar and whisk until it holds stiff peaks, then gently fold into the mascarpone. Spread this in an even layer across the top of the pavlova and top with diced mango. Pour over the seeds and juice from the passion fruit.

CRUNCHY APRICOT PARFAIT

I've included this recipe because when I eat it I am taken straight back to my childhood. This was a dish I always looked forward to when I was little – the dessert I remember asking for again and again. Made with fresh apricots it's a nostalgic summertime treat. It is super easy to put together and tastes absolutely delicious.

SERVES 4

FOR THE APRICOT LAYER
12 SMALL RIPE APRICOTS, HALVED,
    STONED AND QUARTERED
1 TEASPOON VANILLA EXTRACT
20G CASTER SUGAR
45ML WATER

FOR THE CREAM LAYER
200ML DOUBLE CREAM
½ TEASPOON VANILLA EXTRACT

FOR THE CRUNCHY TOPPING
55G BUTTER
110G DARK BROWN SUGAR
50G CORNFLAKES

Put the ingredients for the apricot layer into a medium pan set over medium heat and cook for 15 minutes or until soft. Set aside to cool.

Take four wine glasses and divide the apricot mixture evenly among them. To make the cream layer, whip the cream and vanilla extract together until it forms soft peaks. Divide among the glasses.

To make the topping, melt the butter and sugar in a medium pan over medium heat. Add the cornflakes and mix until evenly combined. Allow to cool slightly before dividing equally among the glasses. Chill.

BANANAS FOSTER PANCAKES

This isn't a classic Bananas Foster — a dessert that originated in New Orleans. For starters, there isn't any ice cream, which is normally thought of as a key ingredient; however, it is based around the same basic ingredients of banana, caramel and rum. I just chose to serve it with pancakes for a comforting dessert or indulgent brunch.

SERVES 4–6

350G SELF-RAISING FLOUR

80G CASTER SUGAR

¼ TEASPOON SALT

2 TEASPOONS BAKING POWDER

4 EGGS

260ML MILK

60G MELTED BUTTER, COOLED, PLUS EXTRA FOR FRYING

2 LARGE BANANAS, SLICED

FOR THE SAUCE

110G BUTTER

110G LIGHT BROWN MUSCOVADO SUGAR

2 TABLESPOONS DOUBLE CREAM

2–3 TABLESPOONS RUM, TO TASTE

In a large bowl, mix the flour, sugar, salt and baking powder together. In a small bowl or jug whisk the eggs and milk together. Whisk in the butter until fully combined.

Pour the milk mixture over the flour, and whisk together until fully combined and smooth. Allow the mixture to rest while you make the sauce.

Melt the butter and sugar together in a medium pan. Once melted and fully combined, stir in the cream and rum. Leave the pan to keep warm over low heat while you make the pancakes.

Heat a frying pan over medium heat, add a knob of butter and allow to melt and bubble. Immediately, pour a small ladleful of batter into the pan to make one pancake. (You can cook two at a time if you are using a large pan.) Cook until the underside is browned and there are a few bubbles on top.

Flip the pancakes over and cook for 1–2 minutes until browned on the underside. Put the cooked pancakes onto a large plate in a warm oven while you cook the remaining batter. Serve with sliced bananas and the caramel rum sauce.

WHITE CHOCOLATE AND MATCHA MOUSSE

This dessert is easy to make but creates an impressive finish to a meal. The slightly unusual white chocolate mousse makes a pleasant change from using the more traditional dark chocolate. The mousse is sweet and light and the ganache underneath is rich with a strong flavour of green tea – a pairing that works really well together. The idea came after I tried a white chocolate and matcha truffle. The flavours worked so well together that I wanted to turn it into a beautiful dessert.

SERVES 6

200G WHITE CHOCOLATE, FINELY CHOPPED
250ML DOUBLE CREAM
2 EGG WHITES
25G CASTER SUGAR

FOR THE MATCHA GANACHE

100G WHITE CHOCOLATE, FINELY CHOPPED
100ML DOUBLE CREAM
1 TEASPOON GREEN TEA POWDER

To make the ganache, put the chocolate in a medium bowl and set aside. Put the cream and green tea powder into a small pan over medium heat and bring just to the boil. Give the cream mixture a good whisk to dissolve the green tea powder, then pour over the chocolate and gently stir together until smooth and glossy.

Divide equally among six glass tumblers or wine glasses and put in the fridge to set while you make the mousse.

Melt the chocolate in the microwave or a heatproof bowl over a pan of gently simmering water, making sure the base of the bowl doesn't touch the water. Set aside to cool a little. Whip the cream to soft peaks and set aside. Put the egg whites into a clean, grease-free bowl (this is best done using a freestanding electric mixer) and whisk until they form firm peaks. With the whisk still on high, gently pour the sugar down the side of the bowl and whisk until the meringue is stiff and glossy.

Mix a third of the meringue mixture into the cream, then gently fold in the remainder. In two additions, gently fold in the white chocolate until just fully combined. Divide equally among the glasses and chill for two hours before serving.

CHOCOLATE POT DE CRÈME

Pot de Crème is a simple baked chocolate custard; it is rich and has a wonderfully deep flavour. I like to make it more exciting by the addition of a little liqueur or fruit. My favourite is the addition of amaretto liqueur to the custard and sprinkling some crumbled amaretti biscuits on top to serve.

SERVES 4

100G CHOCOLATE (AT LEAST
    60–70% COCOA SOLIDS),
    CHOPPED
60ML WHOLE MILK
240ML DOUBLE CREAM
50G CASTER SUGAR
3 EGG YOLKS
PINCH OF SALT
2 TABLESPOONS AMARETTO LIQUEUR
4 AMARETTI BISCUITS, CRUMBLED

Preheat the oven to 170°C (150°C fan oven) gas mark 3. Put the chocolate into a heatproof bowl. In a medium pan set over medium heat bring the milk, cream and sugar to the boil. Pour over the chopped chocolate and whisk until smooth.

In a medium bowl beat the egg yolks together, then slowly pour over the chocolate cream with the salt, whisking gently until fully combined. Stir in the liqueur.

Divide the mixture equally between four ramekins and put them into a roasting pan. Pour water into the pan until it reaches halfway up the ramekins. Bake for 30–35 minutes or until the pots are almost set but still a little wobbly in the centre. Cover and chill for a minimum of 4 hours. Allow to return to room temperature before serving topped with crumbled amaretti biscuits.

TIP
This is a rich dessert and is best served with a little lightly whipped cream.

VARIATION
You could also flavour this with mint extract in place of the amaretto liqueur.

CHOCOLATE MOUSSE WITH BLACKCURRANT COMPOTE

A chocolate mousse is one of those really simple and convenient desserts, and it's possible that you have everything you need to make it already in the cupboard. The blackcurrant compote pairs beautifully with the chocolate but, if you prefer, you could simply top it with fresh raspberries or even just a little cream. Once you have whisked your egg whites, fold them into the chocolate nice and gently, just until you can no longer see them; that way you won't lose the air trapped inside them, and you will have a lovely light dessert.

SERVES 4

85G DARK CHOCOLATE (AT LEAST
  60–70% COCOA SOLIDS), FINELY
  CHOPPED
3 EGGS, SEPARATED
PINCH OF SALT
1 TABLESPOON CASTER SUGAR

FOR THE COMPOTE
150G BLACKCURRANTS
50G CASTER SUGAR
1 TABLESPOON LEMON JUICE

Melt the chocolate in a microwave or heatproof bowl over a pan of gently simmering water, making sure the base of the bowl doesn't touch the water. Take off the heat and beat in the egg yolks and salt.

Put the egg whites into a clean bowl and whisk until foamy, then add the sugar slowly, beating on high speed until stiff and shiny. Beat a third of the whites into the chocolate mixture to lighten it, then gently fold in the remainder. Divide the mousse among four ramekins or glasses and chill for 4 hours.

To make the compote, put the fruit, sugar and lemon juice into a small pan. Over low heat bring to the boil and, when the fruit just starts to pop, remove from the heat and allow to cool. Top the mousses with the blackcurrant compote, and serve.

DULCE DE LECHE BANANA BREAD PUDDING

This delicious twist on a classic American-style bread pudding uses dulce de leche, a thick milk-based caramel, and banana. It's wonderful served with Ginger Crème Anglaise. Whilst it is, of course, wonderful hot, I also love this when it has cooled down, served the next day.

SERVES 8–10

BUTTER, FOR GREASING

1 LARGE BRIOCHE LOAF OR
    CHALLAH (ABOUT 500G)

200G DULCE DE LECHE

2 BANANAS, SLICED

6 EGGS

40G DARK MUSCOVADO SUGAR

400ML MILK

400ML DOUBLE CREAM

GINGER CRÈME ANGLAISE
    (PAGE 164), TO SERVE

Preheat the oven to 180°C (160°C fan oven) gas mark 4 and lightly butter a 23 × 33cm glass baking dish. Slice the brioche or challah into 2cm thick slices. Cut these slices diagonally in half and spread each with a thick layer of dulce de leche and top with a couple of banana slices. Arrange the slices in the prepared dish.

Whisk the eggs and sugar together in a large bowl followed by the milk and cream. Pour this mixture evenly over the brioche slices in the dish. Press the bread lightly so that the custard soaks through completely.

Cover the pudding with foil and bake for 50 minutes, then remove the foil and bake for a further 10–20 minutes or until the middle is just a little wobbly.

BROWN SUGAR PANNACOTTA

Pannacotta is a set cream usually flavoured simply with vanilla. It has a gorgeous silky smooth, melt-in-the-mouth texture. Instead of using caster sugar as is usual, I have opted to use brown sugar here, which gives the pannacotta the most amazing light caramel flavour that works wonderfully with the strawberries infused with a hint of balsamic vinegar.

SERVES 4

2 LEAVES GELATINE

ICE-COLD WATER, FOR SOAKING

1 VANILLA POD

300ML DOUBLE CREAM

200ML WHOLE MILK

50G LIGHT BROWN SUGAR

400G STRAWBERRIES, HULLED AND
  SLICED INTO QUARTERS

2–3 TEASPOONS BALSAMIC VINEGAR
  OR FRUIT VINEGAR

2 TABLESPOONS CASTER SUGAR

Put the gelatine into a small bowl and cover with ice-cold water, then leave to soak for five minutes.

Scrape the seeds from the vanilla pod and put into a medium pan with the cream, milk and sugar. Set over medium heat and bring to a simmer. Remove from the heat and set aside.

Squeeze all the water from the gelatine and add to the cream mixture. Stir to combine. Divide evenly among four small ramekins and chill for a minimum of 4 hours or overnight.

To make the macerated strawberries put the strawberries, vinegar and sugar into a small bowl and mix to combine. Leave to stand for a few hours, adding more vinegar if you like.

To turn out, dip the ramekins in hot water for a few seconds to loosen, then invert onto a serving plate. Serve with strawberries around the pannacottas.

COCONUT CREAM CHEESE FRENCH TOAST

This was an idea that popped into my head when I was wondering what I could do to French toast to make it even more tasty. Although it sounded odd to others at the time, I was convinced that it would be delicious, and it really is. Although the flavours of coconut and cream cheese are normally strong, here they are balanced and are not overpowering. Serve family-style and just let everyone tuck in.

SERVES 4

5 EGGS

250ML COCONUT MILK

SEEDS FROM ONE VANILLA POD OR
   1 TEASPOON VANILLA BEAN PASTE

200G LIGHT CREAM CHEESE

1 TABLESPOON ICING SUGAR

16 THIN (1CM) BRIOCHE SLICES

12 TABLESPOONS DESICCATED
   COCONUT (SWEETENED OR NOT)

VEGETABLE OIL, FOR SHALLOW
   FRYING

SLICED BANANA AND MAPLE SYRUP,
   TO SERVE

Whisk the eggs, coconut milk and vanilla together and pour into a shallow dish.

Mix the cream cheese and icing sugar together and spread evenly over 8 slices of brioche, then sprinkle with a layer of coconut. Sandwich the slices together with a second piece of brioche.

Heat a pan over medium-high heat with a little vegetable oil. Dip the sandwiches in the egg mixture, allowing both sides to soak some in. Fry until browned on both sides then slice diagonally. Serve with sliced banana and maple syrup.

BROWNIE SUNDAE

Delicious desserts don't have to be complicated or difficult, in fact I think it's sometimes better if they are quick and easy, just like this one. If you prefer to buy the brownies, then the rest is a simple as it could possibly be. I have made a classic chocolate sundae but, for variation, you could swap the brownies for blondies or simply change the sauce – it would be delicious with Salted Caramel Sauce (page 153), it's up to you. Have a play and make a version that you would love.

SERVES 4

4 BROWNIES, HOMEMADE (PAGE 48) OR STORE-BOUGHT

4 SCOOPS VANILLA ICE CREAM (PAGE 154)

1 QUANTITY WARM DARK CHOCOLATE SAUCE (PAGE 162)

40G PECANS, ROUGHLY CHOPPED

If the brownies are cold, put them on an ovenproof plate in a warm oven to heat up while you make the sauce.

To assemble and serve the sundaes, put the warmed brownies onto serving plates. Top with a large scoop of ice cream and drizzle with the warm chocolate sauce. Sprinkle with the chopped nuts and serve immediately

VARIATION
Use the Speculaas Blondie recipe (page 51) instead of brownies, and serve with Salted Caramel Sauce (page 153) and chopped hazelnuts.

EDD'IBLE MESS

The inspiration for this dessert comes from Eton Mess: the classic British summertime dessert. Here, I've used raspberries, both puréed and whole, and to highlight their wonderful sweet flavour I've combined them with cream, a little mascarpone and rich, dark chocolate. It's really quite indulgent.

SERVES 4

2 LARGE EGG WHITES

115G CASTER SUGAR

150ML DOUBLE CREAM

60G MASCARPONE

350G RASPBERRIES

1 TABLESPOON LEMON JUICE

2 TABLESPOONS ICING SUGAR,
   OR TO TASTE

60G DARK CHOCOLATE (AT LEAST
   60–70% COCOA SOLIDS), ROUGHLY
   CHOPPED

Preheat the oven to 110°C (90°C fan oven) gas mark ¼ and line a baking tray with baking parchment. Put the egg whites into a clean, grease-free bowl (this is best done using a freestanding electric mixer) and whisk until they form soft peaks.

Slowly pour in the sugar in a slow stream and continue to beat until the meringue is stiff and glossy.

Scoop heaped dessertspoonfuls of the meringue onto the prepared baking tray and bake for 1½–2 hours or until dry and crisp. Turn off the oven and allow the meringues to dry out for 2 hours, or overnight if possible.

Put the double cream and mascarpone into a medium bowl and whisk until it just holds very soft peaks. Purée half the raspberries with the lemon juice and icing sugar and pass through a sieve to remove the seeds.

To assemble the dessert, crumble the meringues with your fingers and gently fold the cream, raspberry purée, whole raspberries, chocolate and meringue together so that each mouthful has a taste of everything but it is not completely mixed together. Divide among four glasses or bowls and serve.

CHOCOLATE AND BANANA BRIOCHE BREAD PUDDING

I grew up with the traditional version of bread and butter pudding, made with sliced white bread, milk, raisins and nutmeg – a very rustic, classic dish. This recipe is more in line with the American version, which is custard-based and richer. It's definitely perfect for a cold autumnal evening.

SERVES 8–10

1 LARGE BRIOCHE LOAF (AT LEAST 500G), PREFERABLY STALE

4 BANANAS, SLICED

400ML WHOLE MILK

400ML WHIPPING CREAM

275G DARK CHOCOLATE (AT LEAST 60–70% COCOA SOLIDS), ROUGHLY CHOPPED

7 EGGS

50G CASTER SUGAR

50G CHOPPED HAZELNUTS

Lightly grease a 23 × 33cm baking dish. Slice the brioche into 1.5cm thick slices and cut into quarters. Put into the prepared pan with the bananas and toss together to combine.

In a large pan heat the milk, cream and 200g of the chocolate until melted and fully combined. In a medium bowl whisk the eggs and sugar together. Bring the milk mixture just to the boil and pour over the eggs, whisking constantly.

Pour the chocolate custard over the brioche and leave to stand for 15 minutes, pressing the bread into the custard occasionally. Preheat the oven to 180°C (160°C fan oven) gas mark 4.

Sprinkle the remaining chocolate over the brioche and press lightly into the mixture. Sprinkle the chopped hazelnuts over the pudding. Bake for 30–35 minutes or until the custard is just set and the filling is golden. Cool for 10 minutes before serving.

ICE CREAMS
AND BASICS

POPCORN ICE CREAM

This may seem a little odd as a flavour for ice cream but, trust me, it really is very good indeed. My favourite way to serve it is with Salted Caramel Sauce (see opposite) and a little chopped chocolate, but it could also be used as a seriously different variation to go in my Baked Alaskas on page 112, using banana and a little caramel sauce to pair with the ice cream.

MAKES ABOUT 1 LITRE

350ML DOUBLE CREAM

400ML MILK

125G CASTER SUGAR

75G POPCORN KERNALS OR 1 PACK
   PLAIN MICROWAVE POPCORN, POPPED

4 EGG YOLKS

1 TEASPOON VANILLA EXTRACT

Put the cream into a medium pan with the milk, 85g of the sugar and the popcorn. Bring to a simmer over medium heat. Remove from the heat and cover the pan for 1 hour to infuse the cream with popcorn flavour. Strain out the popcorn and bring the milk mixture back to a simmer. Discard the popcorn.

As the liquid comes to temperature put the egg yolks, remaining sugar and the vanilla extract into a medium bowl and whisk together. Once the milk mixture has come to a simmer slowly pour it onto the eggs, whisking constantly.

Scrape this mixture back into the pan and put back over low heat and cook, stirring constantly, until the custard thickens enough to coat the back of a wooden spoon.

Fill a large bowl one-third full of water and ice, and put a medium bowl inside to make an ice bath. Pour the custard into the bowl and stir until cooled. Press a piece of clingfilm to the surface of the custard and chill for a minimum of 8 hours.

If using an ice cream maker, churn the custard according to the manufacturer's instructions. Serve or transfer to a freezerproof container and freeze.

If making by hand, transfer to a freezerproof container and freeze for 2 hours. Whisk to break up the ice crystals, then freeze for another 2 hours. Repeat the process twice more.

Allow the ice cream to soften a little before serving.

SALTED CARAMEL SAUCE

This is one of my favourite treats — I can eat this without anything extra, straight from the jar. But if you really must serve it with something else, it works perfectly with ice cream or as part of a sundae. This sauce keeps really well if stored in the fridge in a sealed jar.

MAKES 285ML

150G GRANULATED SUGAR
PINCH OF SEA SALT
125ML DOUBLE CREAM
10G SALTED BUTTER, SOFTENED

In a medium pan melt the sugar over medium heat until dark brown in colour, stopping before it starts to smoke. Remove from the heat and carefully add the salt and pour in half the cream. The mixture will bubble violently so be careful and go slowly.

Once the mixture has settled, add the remaining cream followed by the butter. If the mixture is lumpy, put the pan back on the heat and stir until smooth. Pour into a heatproof jar and leave to cool.

VANILLA
ICE CREAM

Classic vanilla ice cream – nothing says summer to me more than indulging in a cone of ice cream while relaxing on the beach, enjoying the warm summer weather. Ice cream really is easy to make: if you can make custard, then you can make ice cream, because it's exactly the same process. Be careful to keep the hob temperature low and make sure to stir the custard constantly – that way you won't end up with a curdled and lumpy custard. My version has a little hit of vodka to help the ice cream to remain softer when frozen, but you can omit it if you prefer.

MAKES ABOUT 1 LITRE

1 VANILLA POD
400ML DOUBLE CREAM
350ML WHOLE MILK
150G CASTER SUGAR
4 EGG YOLKS
1½ TABLESPOONS VODKA (OPTIONAL)

Split the vanilla pod and scrape out the seeds. Put the cream into a medium pan with the milk, half the sugar, the beans from the vanilla pod and the pod itself. Bring to a simmer over medium heat.

As the liquid comes to temperature put the egg yolks and the remaining sugar into a medium bowl and whisk together. Once the cream mixture has come to a simmer remove the vanilla pod and slowly pour onto the eggs, whisking constantly.

Scrape this mixture back into the pan and put back over low heat. Cook, stirring constantly, until the custard thickens enough to coat the back of a wooden spoon.

Fill a large bowl one-third full of water and ice, and put a medium bowl inside to make an ice bath. Pour the custard into the bowl and stir until cooled. Stir in the vodka, if using, and press a piece of clingfilm to the surface of the custard. Chill for a minimum of 8 hours.

If using an ice cream maker, churn the custard according to the manufacturer's instructions. Serve or transfer to a freezerproof container and freeze.

If making by hand, transfer to a freezerproof container and freeze for 2 hours. Whisk to break up the ice crystals, then freeze for another 2 hours. Repeat the process twice more.

Allow the ice cream to soften a little before serving.

MALT
ICE CREAM

I serve this ice cream with a chocolate or caramel sauce to replicate one of my favourite childhood chocolate bars.

MAKES ABOUT 1 LITRE

300ML DOUBLE CREAM
450ML WHOLE MILK
150G CASTER SUGAR
6 TABLESPOONS MALT POWDER
4 EGG YOLKS
½ TEASPOON VANILLA EXTRACT
1½ TABLESPOONS VODKA (OPTIONAL)

Put the cream into a medium pan with the milk, half the sugar and the malt powder. Bring to a simmer over medium heat, whisking occasionally to help dissolve the malt.

As the liquid comes to temperature, put the egg yolks, the remaining sugar and the vanilla extract into a medium bowl and whisk together. Once the cream mixture has come to a simmer pour it onto the eggs, whisking constantly.

Scrape this mixture back into the pan and put back over low heat. Cook, stirring constantly, until the custard thickens enough to coat the back of a wooden spoon.

Fill a large bowl one-third full of water and ice, and put a medium bowl inside to make an ice bath. Pour the custard into the bowl and stir until cooled. Stir in the vodka, if using, and press a piece of clingfilm to the surface of the custard. Chill for a minimum of 8 hours.

If using an ice cream maker, churn the custard according to the manufacturer's instructions. Serve or transfer to a freezerproof container and freeze.

If making by hand, transfer to a freezerproof container and freeze for 2 hours. Whisk to break up the ice crystals, then freeze for another 2 hours. Repeat the process twice more.

Allow the ice cream to soften a little before serving.

MATCHA
ICE CREAM

The high-quality, finely ground Japanese green tea, matcha, has an interesting flavour that develops from slightly bitter into sweetness and goes very well with cakes and desserts. Not much of this intensely flavoured powder is needed to create a strongly flavoured ice cream. It also tastes great with fresh fruit served with a little white chocolate sauce.

MAKES ABOUT 1 LITRE

350ML DOUBLE CREAM
400ML WHOLE MILK
150G CASTER SUGAR
4 TEASPOONS MATCHA POWDER
4 EGG YOLKS
1½ TABLESPOONS VODKA (OPTIONAL)

Put the cream into a medium pan with the milk, half the sugar and the matcha powder. Bring to a simmer over medium heat, then whisk to allow the matcha powder to dissolve fully.

While the liquid heats, put the egg yolks and remaining sugar into a medium bowl and whisk together. Once the cream mixture is simmering pour it over the eggs, whisking constantly. Scrape this mixture back into the pan and put back over low heat. Cook, stirring constantly, until the custard thickens enough to coat the back of a wooden spoon.

Fill a large bowl one-third full of water and ice, and put a medium bowl inside to make an ice bath. Pour the custard into the bowl and stir until cooled. Stir in the vodka, if using, and press a piece of clingfilm to the surface of the custard. Chill for a minimum of 8 hours.

If using an ice cream maker, churn the custard according to the manufacturer's instructions. Serve or transfer to a freezerproof container and freeze. If making by hand, transfer to a freezerproof container and freeze for 2 hours. Whisk to break up the ice crystals, then freeze for another 2 hours. Repeat the process twice more. Allow the ice cream to soften a little before serving.

NOTE
Matcha powder is available at some supermarkets as well as most Asian supermarkets and online.

LIQUORICE ICE CREAM

I grew up in Yorkshire, not far from Pontefract — the home of Pontefract Cakes, the famous liquorice sweets — and I have always had a soft spot for the stuff. This ice cream may seem odd to some, but it is actually wonderful served with apple crumble. The flavour of liquorice is tempered in the custard so that it isn't as intense as the confection itself but it still retains that wonderful aniseed flavour.

MAKES ABOUT 1 LITRE

450ML DOUBLE CREAM
300ML WHOLE MILK
80G CASTER SUGAR
150G BLACK LIQUORICE
6 EGG YOLKS

Put the cream into a medium pan with the milk, half the sugar and the liquorice. Bring to a simmer over medium heat. Remove from the heat and cover for 1 hour, stirring occasionally. Bring the cream mixture back to a simmer and, if the liquorice hasn't melted completely, use a hand blender to create a smooth mixture.

While the cream mixture simmers, put the egg yolks and the remaining sugar into a medium bowl and whisk together. Pour the cream mixture onto the eggs, whisking constantly.

Scrape this mixture back into the pan, put over low heat and cook, stirring constantly, until the custard thickens enough to coat the back of a wooden spoon.

Fill a large bowl one-third full of water and ice, and put a medium bowl inside to make an ice bath. Pour the custard into the bowl and stir until cooled. Press a piece of clingfilm to the surface of the custard, and chill for a minimum of 8 hours.

If using an ice cream maker, churn the custard according to the manufacturer's instructions. Serve or transfer to a freezerproof container and freeze.

If making by hand, transfer to a freezerproof container and freeze for 2 hours. Whisk to break up the ice crystals, then freeze for another 2 hours. Repeat the process twice more. Allow the ice cream to soften a little before serving.

BLACKBERRY SHERBET

This recipe isn't actually an ice cream but rather a sherbet, a type of sorbet that includes milk. It is the most refreshing way to end a meal and would be perfect on a hot summer's day. It can be made faster and easier than ice cream, but is still full of flavour and also healthier, as it includes no cream. Serve with fresh fruit or compote to make a quick improvised dessert or serve alongside a slice of warm apple pie.

MAKES ABOUT 1 LITRE

200G CASTER SUGAR
250ML MILK
1 TABLESPOON LIQUID GLUCOSE
500G BLACKBERRIES
2 TEASPOONS LEMON JUICE

Put the sugar, milk, glucose and blackberries in a food processor or blender and process until smooth and evenly combined.

Pour the mixture through a fine sieve to remove the seeds. Add the lemon juice and chill the mixture for 1 hour or until cool.

If using an ice cream maker, churn the sherbet according to the manufacturer's instructions. Serve or transfer to a freezerproof container and freeze until needed.

If making by hand, transfer to a freezerproof container and freeze for 4 hours. Blend in a food processor or blender until smooth, then return to the freezer for 4 hours or until needed.

Remove from the freezer a few minutes before serving to allow the sherbet to soften slightly.

ICE CREAMS AND BASICS　[161]

WHITE CHOCOLATE SAUCE

Unjustly I think, white chocolate gets a bad press. Although it's not technically chocolate as it doesn't contain cocoa solids, it has a wonderful creamy texture that I love. When used to complement other flavours it can work very well. Just make sure you buy good-quality chocolate with a high cocoa butter content. Served with Matcha Ice Cream (page 156) and fresh fruit, this white chocolate sauce makes for a delicious quick and easy dessert.

MAKES 275ML

175ML DOUBLE CREAM
100G WHITE CHOCOLATE, (AROUND
   30% COCOA BUTTER) FINELY
   CHOPPED
1 TEASPOON VANILLA EXTRACT

Put the cream and chocolate into a small pan and cook over medium heat, stirring occasionally until the chocolate melts and the sauce is combined.

Stir in the vanilla extract, then pour into a heatproof jug and allow to cool slightly. The longer you leave the sauce the thicker it will get; to thin it out, gently heat it up until it returns to the desired consistency.

DARK CHOCOLATE SAUCE

This sauce is the most decadent, over-the-top sauce ever, but it's so worth the effort. It's amazing with the Brownie Sundae (page 144), especially if you use homemade brownies, and of course it transforms simple Vanilla Ice Cream (page 154) into something completely different! This recipe makes quite a lot, so just halve it if you want less.

MAKES 500ML

150G DARK CHOCOLATE (AT LEAST
   60–70% COCOA SOLIDS)
15G BUTTER
2 TABLESPOONS HONEY
300ML DOUBLE CREAM

Put the chocolate, butter, honey and cream into a small pan and cook over medium heat, stirring occasionally, until the chocolate melts and the sauce is smooth and fully combined.

Pour into a heatproof jug and allow to cool slightly. The longer you leave the sauce the thicker it will get; to thin it out, gently heat it up until it returns to the desired consistency.

CRÈME ANGLAISE

Crème Anglaise is a thin pouring custard that is perfect for crumbles or fruit pies. As it is flavoured simply with vanilla, it is nice to use a real vanilla pod instead of extract so that you get a more intense result. If you can't get hold of pods, then substitute it with 2 teaspoons vanilla extract or 1 teaspoon vanilla bean paste.

MAKES 600ML

1 VANILLA POD
500ML WHOLE MILK
5 EGG YOLKS
40G CASTER SUGAR

Scrape the seeds from the vanilla pod and put the seeds and pod into a medium pan. Add the milk and bring to a simmer over medium heat.

Put the egg yolks and sugar into a medium bowl and whisk together until pale and slightly thickened.

Pour the milk through a sieve over the eggs and whisk together. Pour back into the pan and cook over low heat, stirring constantly, until it thickens enough to coat the back of a wooden spoon. Pour into a heatproof jug to serve.

GINGER CRÈME ANGLAISE

If you want a custard with more flavour, why not try this ginger version? It goes particularly well with the Dulce de Leche Banana Bread Pudding (page 138) or poured over Individual Apple Crumbles (page 126).

MAKES 600ML

500ML WHOLE MILK
25G ROOT GINGER, PEELED AND
  ROUGHLY CHOPPED
40G CASTER SUGAR
5 EGG YOLKS

Put the milk and ginger into a medium pan and bring to a simmer over medium heat. Cover the pan with a lid and leave to infuse for 30 minutes.

In a medium bowl, beat the sugar and egg yolks together until pale and thickened. Put the milk back on the heat and bring back to a simmer. Pour the milk through a sieve over the eggs and whisk together.

Pour back into the pan and cook over low heat, stirring constantly, until it thickens enough to coat the back of a wooden spoon. Pour into a heatproof jug to serve.

PASTRY CREAM

Pastry cream, or *crème pâtissière* as it's properly known, is a custard made with flour or cornflour so that it thickens. Traditionally, it is used to fill all sorts of patisserie, from eclairs to doughnuts. Here is the classic vanilla, and I've also provided a chocolate-flavoured version too.

MAKES 400G

300ML WHOLE MILK
4 EGG YOLKS
1 TABLESPOON PLAIN FLOUR
30G CASTER SUGAR
1 TEASPOON VANILLA EXTRACT

In a medium pan bring the milk to a simmer over medium heat. Meanwhile, whisk the egg yolks, flour and sugar together in a medium bowl.

Once the milk has come to temperature, slowly pour half of it over the egg mixture, whisking constantly. Scrape the egg mixture back into the pan and cook over medium heat until thickened, whisking constantly. Pour into a bowl and stir in the vanilla. Press a piece of clingfilm to the surface of the custard and chill until needed.

CHOCOLATE PASTRY CREAM

If you fancy something a little more indulgent than the classic pastry cream, give this chocolate version a whirl. You could even use it to make a delicious chocolate trifle.

300ML WHOLE MILK
50G DARK CHOCOLATE (AT LEAST 60–70% COCOA SOLIDS), FINELY CHOPPED
4 EGG YOLKS
1 TABLESPOON COCOA POWDER
1 TABLESPOON PLAIN FLOUR
30G SUGAR
1 TEASPOON VANILLA EXTRACT

In a medium pan bring the milk and chocolate to a simmer over medium heat, whisking occasionally to combine the melting chocolate. Meanwhile, whisk the egg yolks, cocoa powder, flour and sugar together in a medium bowl.

Once the milk has come to temperature, slowly pour half of it over the egg mixture, whisking constantly. Scrape the egg mixture back into the pan and cook over medium heat until thickened, whisking constantly. Pour into a bowl and stir in the vanilla. Press a piece of clingfilm to the surface of the custard and chill until needed.

FRUIT COMPOTES

Fresh fruit compotes are a very simple way to dress up ice cream for an improvised dessert. You can use all sorts of fruit, such as apples, plums and raspberries – pretty much whatever you can get your hands on. I have provided a few ideas here, but the method holds true for all fruit. Adjust the sugar level depending on the sweetness of the fruit you are using, and cook until the fruit softens, but stop before it becomes mushy, as it needs to retain some texture. You could also add other flavourings, such as vanilla extract or spices; cinnamon in a pear compote is a good combination.

MAKES 200G

150G BLACKCURRANTS
50G SUGAR
1 TABLESPOON LEMON JUICE

BLACKCURRANT COMPOTE

Put the fruit, sugar and lemon juice into a small pan. Over low heat bring to a gentle boil and, when the fruit just starts to pop, remove from the heat and allow it to cool. Stored in sterilised jars, the compote will keep for a few days in the fridge.

MAKES 500G

350G REDCURRANTS
150G SUGAR
ZEST OF 1 ORANGE
JUICE OF ½ LEMON

REDCURRANT COMPOTE

Put the fruit, sugar, orange zest and lemon juice into a small pan. Bring to a gentle boil over low heat and, when the fruit just starts to pop, remove from the heat and allow to cool. Stored in sterilized jars, the compote will keep for a few days in the fridge.

LEMON CURD

Pure sunshine in a jar! Lemon curd is full of bright, zingy flavours, perfect for spreading on a scone or even simply on toast. Once poured into sterilised jars it will keep perfectly in the fridge for two weeks.

MAKES 450G

ZEST OF 1 LEMON
85ML LEMON JUICE, ABOUT 3
   LEMONS
175G SUGAR
5 LARGE EGG YOLKS
100G BUTTER, SOFTENED AND
   CUT INTO PIECES

Put the zest, juice and sugar into a medium pan and whisk in the egg yolks. Cook over low heat, stirring constantly, until the mixture thickens enough to coat the back of a wooden spoon.

Pour into a medium bowl and stir in the butter, a few pieces at a time. Pour into a sterilised jar and chill until needed.

FLAKY PASTRY

This recipe is useful when you want a pastry that is flakier than shortcrust but you want something faster than the Rough Puff Pastry recipe on page 172. I use it as the basis of my Ceccles Cakes (page 83), but it would be equally delicious filled with a chunky apple compote to make a quick apple turnover.

MAKES ABOUT 1KG

600G PLAIN FLOUR
PINCH OF SALT
400G BUTTER, CHILLED AND
    CUT INTO SMALL PIECES

Put the flour and salt into the bowl of a food processor and pulse to combine. Add the butter and pulse until the mixture resembles uneven breadcrumbs, a few lumps here and there is perfect.

Add 3–4 tablespoons cold water and pulse until the mixture just begins to hold together. Tip out onto the work surface and, using your hands, lightly bring the dough together into a ball, making sure to avoid working it too much. Form the dough into a disk and chill for 30 minutes before use.

(Alternatively, make it by hand. Sift the flour and salt into a large bowl. Add the butter and quickly rub it in using your fingertips or a pastry blender until it resembles uneven breadcrumbs, a few lumps here and there is perfect.

Add 3–4 tablespoons cold water and, using a palette knife, start to bring it together. Once it just begins to hold together, tip it out onto the work surface and proceed as above.)

SWEET PASTRY

This pastry is perfect for tarts. It is rich, sweet and, if handled correctly, it is also crisp but tender. To ensure the correct texture, it is essential not to overwork the dough, because the more you do, the tougher the pastry will be. You also want to keep everything cool, because if the pastry gets too warm the butter will melt and you will end up with a poor-quality result. A food processor is perfect for achieving the desired texture; it enables you to work fast and stops your hands overworking or overheating the dough.

MAKES ABOUT 1KG

550G PLAIN FLOUR

50G GROUND ALMONDS

100G ICING SUGAR

½ TEASPOON SALT

SEEDS FROM 1 VANILLA POD

350G UNSALTED BUTTER

2 EGG YOLKS

2 TABLESPOONS ICED WATER

Pulse the flour, ground almonds, icing sugar and salt together in a food processor to combine. Scrape the seeds from the vanilla pod and add to the flour mixture.

Pulse the butter into the flour until it resembles coarse, not fine, breadcrumbs – a few lumps are fine.

Mix together the egg yolks and the iced water and add to the mixture, pulsing until the dough just starts to come together. If it isn't coming together, add more water, little by little, until it does.

Tip the dough onto the work surface and knead lightly until just uniform. Flatten into two discs and wrap in clingfilm. Chill for at least 30 minutes or until ready to use.

(Alternatively, you can make this pastry the traditional way by hand. Mix all the dry ingredients together in a large bowl and, using your fingertips or a pastry blender, rub in the butter until it resembles coarse, uneven breadcrumbs. Mix the yolks and the iced water together and add to the bowl, mixing until the dough just comes together, then tip out onto the work surface and continue as above.)

SHORTCRUST PASTRY

This is my version of classic shortcrust pastry recipe, which is perfect for pies, especially those filled with fruit such as the Streusel Apple Pie (page 111). It has a wonderfully light, melt-in-the-mouth texture that I would happily eat in any sort of pie.

MAKES ABOUT 700G

250G UNSALTED BUTTER, DICED
    AND CHILLED
400G PLAIN FLOUR
1 TEASPOON SALT
70–125ML ICED WATER

In a large bowl, rub the butter into the flour and salt with your fingertips, or using a pastry blender, until it resembles irregular breadcrumbs, making sure that there are some slightly larger lumps.

Tip the flour mixture onto the work surface and make a well into the centre. Add half the water and mix until the mixture starts to come together, adding more water if the mixture is too dry. Using the heel of your hand, press and smear the dough across the work surface a few times, then gather it together and form into two flat rounds. Wrap in clingfilm and chill for 30 minutes.

(Alternatively, you can make the pastry in a food processor by pulsing the flour, salt and butter until the mixture resembles irregular breadcrumbs. Add the water and pulse until the dough just starts to come together. Tip the mixture out onto the work surface and proceed as above.)

ROUGH PUFF PASTRY

Puff pastry is the flakiest and most delicious of doughs but it also requires the most time to make. This rough version has much of the characteristic rise and taste of puff pastry but it takes considerably less time to make.

MAKES ABOUT 600G

150G PLAIN FLOUR, PLUS EXTRA
  FOR DUSTING
PINCH OF SALT
150G UNSALTED BUTTER, CHILLED
  AND CUT INTO SMALL PIECES
60ML ICED WATER
2 TEASPOONS LEMON JUICE

Sift the flour and salt onto the work surface and make a well in the centre. Add the butter and use your fingers to work it into the flour until flaky. Do not rub in completely as you would with a shortcrust – you need to leave flaky chunks of butter visible.

Gradually work in the water and lemon juice until the mixture comes together as a rough dough. Gather it into a ball, then wrap in clingfilm and chill for 20 minutes.

On a lightly floured surface, roll the dough into a 4mm thick rectangle. Fold the short ends over the middle, in thirds like a letter, and turn the dough through 90 degrees so that the folds are facing forwards. Roll the dough out again into a 4mm thick rectangle and repeat the folding process. Wrap the dough in clingfilm and chill for a further 20 minutes.

Repeat the rolling as above twice more, then chill the dough until needed.

INDEX

ACKNOWLEDGEMENTS

Writing this book has been one of the most fun, rewarding and exciting projects I have ever worked on and there are a lot of people that I want to thank, who have helped turn my ideas and recipes into something I am tremendously proud of.

Firstly and probably most importantly I want to thank my parents for being supportive and inspiring. They always made me believe that I could follow my dreams and pursue my passion – this book would never have happened if it wasn't for them.

The rest of my family and to my friends for being willing recipe and idea testers. Whenever I had a cake that needed critiquing or an idea I needed to bounce off someone, there was always someone willing to help. My brother Simon especially, who managed to survive living with me whilst I took over the kitchen, day and night, for giving me great feedback and always being there with a helping hand.

To Matt, for being my biggest champion and a massive support – whenever I was doubting something or needed someone to just read through some text you were there. I couldn't ask for a better boyfriend, or a better friend, you helped make writing this book the most amazing experience and I'm so glad you were there with me.

To Kyle and Judith who loved my idea from the start and gave me the opportunity to fulfil my dream of writing a cookbook, and to Catharine for being a wonderful editor who helped bring my ideas to life. To Stuart and everyone at MyJam – thanks for helping me in the last year and for seeing the potential for a book.

To Yuki for being an amazing photographer, I couldn't have asked for someone nicer to work with – your pictures brought my recipes to life in the most beautiful way. Cynthia and Bianca thanks for making the feel of the book just perfect, you got the idea I had and helped create the book I wanted. To Georgia for creating the final look for the book, which I love, and Jan for making sure my words and recipes made sense.

Finally I want to thank the BBC and Love Productions as well as Paul Hollywood and Mary Berry, who saw my potential and gave me the biggest opportunity of my life, and Gail and Arianna, amongst others, who persuaded me to apply in the first place.